TOP 10 PROVENCE

AND THE CÔTE D'AZUR

CONTENTS

4

Introducing Provence and the Côte d'Azur

18

Top 10 Highlights

PROVENCE AND THE CÔTE D'AZUR

INTRODUCING

Picturesque Moustiers-Sainte-Marie

WELCOME TO PROVENCE AND THE CÔTE D'AZUR

With its blooming lavender fields, masterpiece-packed art galleries and golden sandy beaches, Provence is one of France's most alluring regions. Don't want to miss a thing? With Top 10 Provence and the Côte d'Azur, you'll enjoy the very best it has to offer.

Travellers have been drawn to this region for centuries, today numbering over 30 million a year. They're as captivated by the glamour of St-Tropez as they are the winding streets of Nice and the buzzing bars of multicultural Marseille. Great art is another highlight here, not least because Provence was once home to artists like Henri Matisse and Marc Chagall. Pieces by

The lush Jardin Exotique in Èze

them, and many others, are on display in the region's world-class art museums; Nice alone has three, with more found in the likes of elegant Aix-en-Provence and hilltop St-Paul-de-Vence. There's history in abundance, too: Roman heritage is found in Arles and Vaison-la-Romaine, while Provence's papal past is on show at Avignon's Palais des Papes.

With so much to see and do, it's good to schedule in relaxation time, something easily found in Provence's great outdoors. Glide across the turquoise waters of the Gorges du Verdon, spy pink flamingos in the Camargue delta or admire pretty purple fields of lavender around the 12th-century Abbaye Notre-Dame de Sénanque. Other delights include beach-lined islands and beautiful terraced gardens. And for those who love to eat and drink, there's plenty of choice, from iconic dishes such as bouillabaisse to lesser-known options like crispy *socca* (chickpea pancakes), all washed down with a glass of the region's excellent wines.

So, where to start? With Top 10 Provence and the Côte d'Azur, of course. This pocket-sized guide gets to the heart of the region with simple lists of 10, expert local knowledge and comprehensive maps, helping you turn an ordinary trip into an extraordinary one.

THE STORY OF **PROVENCE AND THE CÔTE D'AZUR**

Provence was one of the first places in France to have been inhabited by humans. In the thousands of years that followed, the region has been part of the Roman Empire, a seat of papal power, a hub for artists, and a glamorous holiday destination. Here's the story of how it came to be.

Prehistoric Provence

Excavations at places like Grotte du Vallonnet in Roquebrune-Cap-Martin suggest that some of the first humans in France lived in Provence, creating tools from stone. These communities also created early forms of art, with the Grotte Cosquer near Marseille peppered with cave paintings of handprints and animals that date from between 33,000 and 19,000 BCE. It is likely these communities became the Ligures, a group who also lived across parts of northern and central Italy. From the 8th century BCE, Celts first clashed, then merged with the Ligures, and the resulting Celtic-Ligurian culture lasted until the Roman conquest in the 2nd century BCE.

Greek and Roman Settlers

In 600 BCE, Greek settlers from Phocaea in Asia Minor founded Massalia – now Marseille – with the city becoming a major trading power in alliance with Rome. It maintained its independence until the first century BCE, when Roman forces arrived and took control. During this time, the Romans also built amphitheatres and arenas at Arles, Orange and Vaison-la-Romaine, among other places, and named the region Provincia Romana (Roman Province), which evolved over time into Provence. The fall of the Roman Empire in 476 CE marked the beginning of a period of instability, with a mix of players tussling over the area, including Germanic tribes,

18th-century depiction of Arles, with its Roman amphitheatre

Roman forces victorious in the Battle of Aquae Sextiae, 102 BCE

Arabs and the Counts of Burgundy. By the 12th century, the Counts of Provence had taken control, making Aix-en-Provence their capital and ruling over a stormy, semi-independent state.

Papal Power Arrives

Provence became part of the new Holy Roman Empire in the 11th century, although it continued to be ruled by the nobility during this time. In 1309, the papacy – abandoning a war-torn Italy – transferred the seat of papal power from Rome to Avignon, making Provence the centre of the Roman Catholic world for over 60 years. During this time the impressive Palais des Papes was constructed, becoming home to seven consecutive popes. The city's reign was temporary, however, and in 1377, Pope Gregory XI restored the papal capital in Rome.

In 1481, following the death of its last ruling count, René the Good, parts of Provence were absorbed into the kingdom of France. The region was thus drawn into 16th-century wars between France and the Habsburg Empire, and into the Wars of Religion (1562–98). This latter conflict, fought between Catholics and "heretic" Protestants, was a turbulent time in Provence due to the region's strong Catholic heritage, with a wave of massacres and the destruction of churches and their contents. While Avignon and other key cities remained staunchly Catholic, others, including Orange, were Huguenot (French Protestant).

Moments in History

1.2 million years BCE
Hominis (early humans) live in Roquebrune-Cap-Martin, alongside prehistoric animals.

600 BCE
Greek settlers from Phocaea found Marseille and plant the first vines in Provence.

476 CE
The Roman Empire falls, leaving a divided Provence tussled over by several groups, among them Arabs and Germanic tribes.

1309
The first of seven popes take the papal seat in Avignon, the newly appointed capital of the Roman Catholic Church.

1481
Much of the region is incorporated into the Kingdom of France, with the devolved parliament in Aix-en-Provence ruled by the Counts of Provence.

1789
Aix-en-Provence loses its status as regional capital in the French Revolution and is demoted to subprefecture.

1860
Nice, Menton and Roquebrune-Cap-Martin are incorporated into Provence (and therefore France) under Napoléon III.

1869
The railway arrives in Nice, paving the way for more tourists to visit the city and the wider region.

1942–44
Occupied Provence sees artists like Matisse escape the big cities to set up base in enclaves like Vence.

2024
Marseille hosts sailing, windsurfing, kite foil and football during the 2024 Paris Olympics.

Artwork depicting the 1860 Treaty of Turin

Revolution and Railways

Towards the end of the 18th century, discontent with France's ruling classes grew and in 1789 the French Revolution took place. It was a pivotal moment countrywide, with peasants in Provence pillaging châteaux and monasteries. The following decades saw the region grow in maritime importance; by the early 19th century, Toulon had become the naval springboard for France's empire in North Africa, while trade with newly conquered territories turned the city of Marseille into a "port of empire".

In the mid-19th century, the first railways from Paris opened, stopping in places like Avignon and Marseille. This, and the sunny climate of the Côte d'Azur, began to attract more and more visitors, with grand hotels and villas built throughout the area. Provence also expanded during this time: Menton and Roquebrune-Cap-Martin were sold to France, both having enjoyed a brief stint as free cities, and Nice – which had yo-yoed between Savoyard and French territory – was ceded to France in the 1860 Treaty of Turin. In 1869 the railway arrived in Nice, causing an even greater uptick of visitors to the region.

An Artistic Awakening

Although France suffered huge losses during World War I, Provence itself was far from the fighting on the Western Front. When peace came, the Côte d'Azur resumed its earlier boomtime, with artists in particular drawn to the area for its quality of light. Among them was Henri Matisse, who spent many years in Nice, and Pablo Picasso, who travelled widely around the region, painting Avignon, Sorgues, Ménerbes and many other Provençal towns and villages.

This period of prosperity ended with the arrival of World War II, with Provence occupied by German troops in 1942. The region was liberated by Allied forces, who landed near St-Tropez, two years later. After the war, holiday-makers returned to the region, among them more artists such as Marc Chagall, who spent time in St-Paul-de-Vence. Provence's reputation for both creativity and glamour was further bolstered in 1946, when it hosted the Cannes Film Festival.

Artist Henri Matisse photographed in 1913

Provence and the Côte d'Azur Today

The region continues to be famed for its beautiful beaches, charming villages and dynamic cities, among them Marseille, the port of arrival for numerous immigrants and one of France's most multicultural places. Provence is also the third-richest region in France thanks to industries like engineering and agriculture. Tourism is also a big earner, with expanded airports and high-speed train lines drawing more tourists to the region than ever before. In fact, Provence today welcomes over 30 million visitors, making it the second most visited place in France after Paris. This has, however, led to concerns of overtourism in some areas, especially at popular natural sites like the Gorges du Verdon and the *calanques* southeast of Marseille. Attempts are being made to address this issue, with visitor numbers now capped in places like the *calanques*.

Nice's Promenade des Anglais at sunset

TOP 10 EXPERIENCES

Planning the perfect trip to Provence and the Côte d'Azur? Whether you're visiting for the first time or making a return trip, there are some things you simply shouldn't miss out on. To make the most of your time – and to enjoy the very best this region has to offer – be sure to add these experiences to your list.

1 Go paddling

Few spots rival Provence for water-based adventures. Kayak the coastal *calanques (p82)* between Cassis and Marseille, gliding past white cliffs and sandy coves. Inland, the Gorges du Verdon *(p24)*, Europe's deepest canyon, has turquoise water that you can skim across by canoe, kayak or paddleboard.

2 Delve into history

Provence has an incredibly rich history. Encounter Roman sights in the likes of Vaison-la-Romaine *(p36)* and Roman Arles *(p28)* – the latter is the site of a spectacular arena – or explore Avignon's papal past at the magnificent Palais des Papes *(p22)*, home to seven successive popes in the 14th century.

3 Admire art

Artists have long flocked to pretty Provence, among them Cézanne, whose studio *(p29)* in Aix-en-Provence can be visited, and Matisse, who fell in love with Nice; the Musée Matisse *(p101)* pays homage to his work. Chagall, meanwhile, adored St-Paul-de-Vence *(p40)*, now home to the Fondation Maeght *(p48)*.

4 Stroll through Vieux Nice

Nice's old town *(p30)* is the perfect place for a wander, thanks to its narrow streets lined with charming Baroque buildings that look as though they've absorbed centuries of sunshine. Dotted here and there are galleries, craft workshops and restaurants serving delicious Provençal cooking.

5 See lavender bloom

From mid-June to early August, swathes of Provence are covered with blooming lavender. For some of the best views of these purple fields, head to the 12th-century Abbaye Notre-Dame de Sénanque *(p38)* or visit hillside Sault during its Fête de la Lavande *(p53)*.

6 Party in Marseille

Often likened to Berlin, France's coolest city has some incredible nightlife, with plenty of rooftop bars and warehouse raves on offer. Watch the sunset with a cocktail in hand at buzzing R2 Le Rooftop *(p84)*, or dance till dawn at edgy L'art-haché *(p84)*.

7 Hit the slopes

After a snowy adrenaline rush? Head to the mountains. Here, there are plenty of great skiing and snowboarding areas *(p62)*, including Le Sauze in the Ubaye valley, La Foux in the Allos valley, and Isola 2000 *(p118)* in the Alpes-Maritimes; the latter offers glimpses of the sea.

8 Enjoy some luxury

The glitzy Côte d'Azur is famed for high-end living. Highlights include St-Tropez *(p32)*, where you can luxuriate on glamorous beaches, and Monaco *(p106)*, known for its superyacht-filled port and legendary Casino de Monte Carlo *(p107)*.

9 Sample local cuisine

The region has lots of delicious dishes *(p68)*, many prepared with seasonal, local ingredients. Don't miss hearty ratatouille, classic bouillabaisse or crispy *socca*. For dessert, try creamy *tarte Tropézienne* and squidgy *calissons d'Aix*.

10 Go wildlife watching

Provence is bursting with wildlife. In the salt flats of the Camargue *(p34)* spot the likes of pink flamingos, wild white horses and black bulls, or journey into the mountains of Parc National du Mercantour *(p56)*, where marmots whistle and chamois roam.

ITINERARIES

Admiring art in Nice, exploring gardens in Menton, dancing till dawn in Marseille: there's a lot to see and do in Provence. With places to eat, shop or simply take in the view, these itineraries offer ways to spend 2 days and 7 days in the region.

2 DAYS IN MARSEILLE

Day 1

Morning
Begin your exploration of Marseille with breakfast at 7VB *(p85)* – the cinnamon brioche here is legendary. Next, stroll through Le Panier *(p81)*, the city's oldest quarter; its streets feature pastel-coloured buildings and street art. From here, it's a 10-minute walk to MuCEM *(p81)*, a futuristic building on the water's edge. Explore its collection, which traces Mediterranean civilization from ancient times to the present day.

Afternoon
With your stomach rumbling, take the scenic oceanside route to the Vieux Port *(p80)* for a long lunch at Placette *(p85)*. This all-day café-bistro offers delicious dishes like octopus fricassee paired with natural wines. After, browse some of the area's excellent shops, before taking a 15-minute stroll to hilltop Notre-Dame de la Garde *(p81)*; its gilded and frescoed interior, complete with pinstriped brickwork, is a delight to explore. As evening arrives, grab dinner at Le Populo *(p85)*, an open-air food court offering everything from Indian to Moroccan food, before heading to R2 Le Rooftop *(p84)* to watch the sunset over the sea, pastis in hand, before dancing the night away.

SHOP
Close to the Vieux Port is L'Herboristerie du Père Blaize *(4 et 6 rue Méolan et du Père Blaize)*, a family-run herbalist with cabinets full of dried plants and flowers.

Vibrant street in Le Panier with alfresco dining

Day 2

Morning
Fuel up for the day at Pollux *(15 Rue d'Isoard)*. This light and bright café serves up excellent coffee and tasty bites, including traditional *viennoiseries* (breakfast pastries). A five-minute walk from here is Palais Longchamp *(p82)*, a 19th-century water tower fronted by two cascading fountains. Admire its

grand architecture before popping into the city's Fine Arts Museum, housed in one of the two adjoining wings. Its vast collection contains over 8,000 paintings, sculptures and drawings dating from the 16th to the 19th centuries. After, take a relaxing amble through the surrounding leafy gardens of the palace.

Afternoon

As afternoon arrives, take the metro and then the bus to Le Petit Nice Passedat *(Anse de Maldormé, Corniche J F Kennedy)*, where you can treat yourself to a Michelin-starred seafood lunch and glorious sea views. Then board the same bus to continue further along the coast to place Amiral Muselier, a short walk from Prado Beaches *(p82)*. Built on reclaimed land, this golden arc of sand is popular with locals, who come to swim, sunbathe and enjoy watersports. Join them for the afternoon and then, as evening arrives, head back into town and make for Belle de Mai. A former tobacco manufacturing district turned artsy quarter, it is home to friendly Le Bar Jo *(p84)* where you can enjoy a great-value dinner and drinks.

TRANSPORT

While Marseille is walkable, it's also hilly. Save your energy for sightseeing by using one of its pay-per-use e-bikes, Le Vélo *(p73)*, or the excellent public transport system *(p140)*. Top tip? A Marseille CityPass *(p145)* includes free public transport.

7 DAYS IN PROVENCE

Day 1

Begin your trip through Provence at the Gorges du Verdon *(p24)*, where huge limestone cliffs frame the Verdon river. The best way to admire these geological giants is by kayak; hire one with the excellent Verdon Canoe *(verdoncanoe.com)*. After, explore the winding streets of Moustiers-Sainte-Marie *(p123)*; visit the hilltop Chapelle Notre-Dame-de-Beauvoir and the Musée de la Faïence, showcasing the town's famous pottery. Then, check into Le Moulin du Château *(p149)*, your home for a two-night stay.

Day 2

Continue exploring the Parc Naturel Régional du Verdon *(p125)* with a 4.5-km (3-mile) round hike from Moustiers-Sainte-Marie, through olive groves, to Belvédère du Tréguier, a viewpoint with panoramic vistas over Lac de Ste-Croix. A 30-minute drive away, in the town of Quinson, is the Musée de Préhistoire des Gorges du Verdon *(p124)*, where you can explore ancient regional history.

Day 3

There's a lot of ground to cover today, so rise early and make the hour's drive to Villecroze *(p94)*. The caves here date from the last Ice Age and were used in the 10th century as refuges during Saracen raids. Perfume capital Grasse is the next stop, 90 minutes away. Visit the Musée du Parfum *(p119)* in the Fragonard factory – one of the town's oldest perfumeries – to learn all about the history of this sweet-smelling art. La Bastide St-Antoine *(p121)*, just south, offers a comfy bed for the night.

Smelling perfumes at the Musée du Parfum, Grasse

Day 4

Today is all about exploring Nice, just a 30-minute drive away. Start with a walk along waterside promenade des Anglais *(p101)*, ending in Vieux Nice *(p30)*, the city's historic heart. There's

EAT

Drop by Tourtour *(p96)* – found between Villecroze and Grasse – for lunch at La Mimounia *(6 rue Grande)*. This family-run spot serves up generous helpings of Moroccan food, including an aromatic lamb tagine, and friendly service.

a maze of narrow streets to explore here, but don't miss rue St-François de Paule, lined with artisan shops. North lies the Musée National Marc Chagall *(p48)*, opened by the artist himself on his 86th birthday and filled with the world's largest collection of his works. As evening arrives, check into the Hôtel du Couvent *(p148)*, your base for the rest of the trip.

Day 5

Medieval St-Paul-de-Vence has been the haunt of artists since the 1920s, and with its winding streets and Riviera views, it's not hard to see why. Start your day trip here by walking the town's 16th-century ramparts *(p40)*, before popping into La Chapelle Folon *(p40)*, a beautiful building dotted with works by Belgian artist Jean-Michel Folon. More art awaits at the Fondation Maeght *(p48)*, home to a vast 20th-century collection (it's one of the largest in Europe).

Day 6

A 30-minute drive from Nice is glitzy Monaco *(p106)*, haunt of the rich and famous. First stop is the lavish Prince's Palace, seat of Monaco's royalty; visit the grand apartments and watch the changing of the guard (11.55am daily). After, snoop at the port's plethora of superyachts, then nip into the leafy Japanese Garden *(p111)*, known for its tranquil ponds and carefully cultivated trees. Finish off the day by popping by the iconic Casino de Monte Carlo *(p107)*.

Day 7

For your last day, head over to Menton. This town, famed for its lemons, is home to Musée Jean Cocteau *(p49)*, the collection of famed poet, playwright, author and film director Jean Cocteau. It's been a busy week, so spend some time afterwards relaxing in the Jardin Botanique Val Rahmeh *(p111)*, a verdant spot dotted with lotus-filled pools and boasting staggering sea views.

Admiring the town of Menton

TOP 10 HIGHLIGHTS

Église St-Trophime, Roman Arles

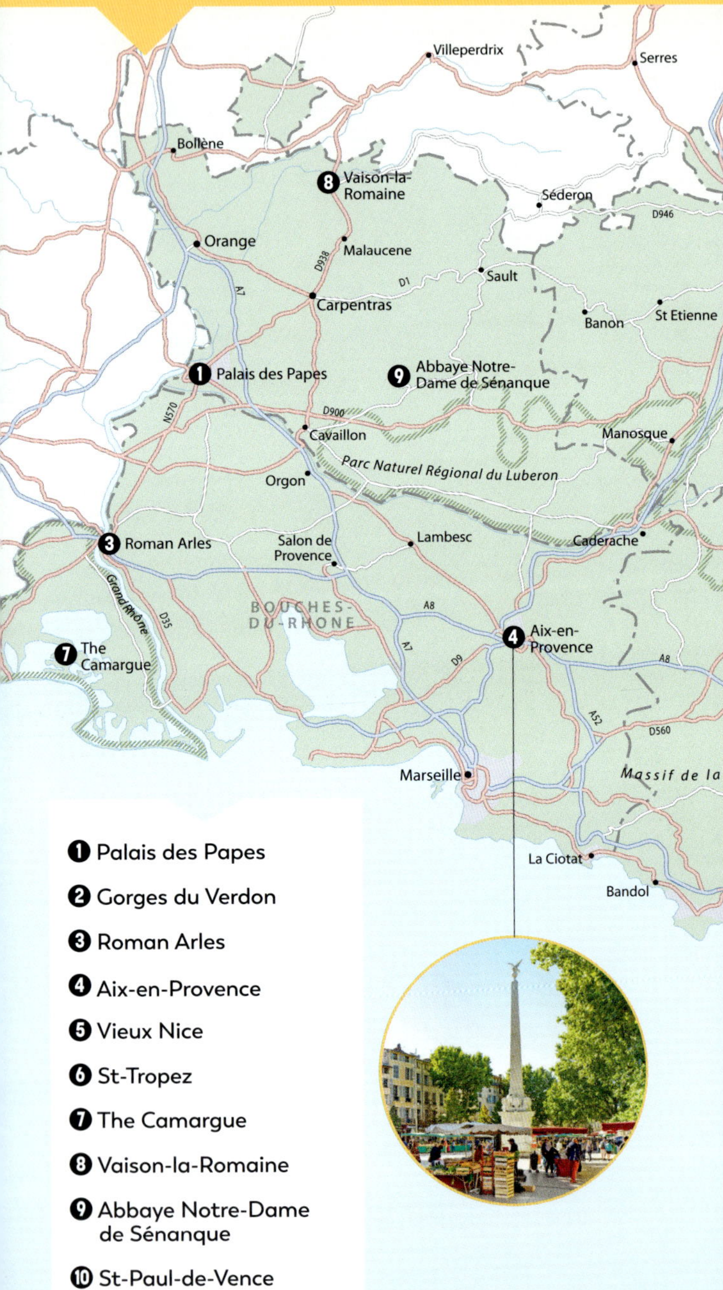

1 Palais des Papes

2 Gorges du Verdon

3 Roman Arles

4 Aix-en-Provence

5 Vieux Nice

6 St-Tropez

7 The Camargue

8 Vaison-la-Romaine

9 Abbaye Notre-Dame de Sénanque

10 St-Paul-de-Vence

EXPLORE THE **HIGHLIGHTS**

There are some sights in Provence and the Côte d'Azur you simply shouldn't miss, and it's these attractions that make the Top 10. Discover what makes each one a must-see on the following pages.

PALAIS DES PAPES

B3 · Pl du Palais, Avignon · Hours vary, check website
palais-des-papes.com

A reminder of the power of the papacy, this 14th-century palace soars above Avignon. Its construction began in 1335, 26 years after Pope Clement V moved the papacy to Avignon to escape political turmoil in Rome. Pope Benedict XII commissioned the Cistercian architecture of the Palais Vieux; his successor, Clement VI, added the Palais Neuf in Gothic style, creating a flamboyant ensemble of turrets and stone walls.

1 Courtyard of Honour

This courtyard is where the two palaces "meet", making it the ideal place to compare their respective styles. While the Old Palace resembles a keep, the New Palace has finer stonework. Today, the courtyard hosts theatrical events during the Avignon Festival *(p74)*.

2 Consistory Hall

The pope, cardinals and dignitaries gathered in the impressive Salle du Consistoire to deliberate on key issues of the day. The hall now serves as a museum of artifacts, housing elegant 14th-century frescoes by Simone Martini.

3 St John's Chapel

Just off the premises of the Consistory Hall, this decorative chapel was created by Matteo Giovanetti, a well-known Sienese artist. The frescoes inside depict the lives of St John the Baptist and St John the Evangelist, with exceptional use of perspective across the walls and the arched vault.

SHOP

Don't miss the souvenir shop in the palace, where local products are offered, including a variety of items such as hand-made ceramic tiles and bottles of wine.

4 Refectory

It was in the large refectory (*tinel*) that the pope entertained on feast days such as a cardinal's appointment or a papal coronation. The pope would eat alone on a dais, while the cardinals and other guests were arranged around the room according to their rank. Its

Exterior of the Palais des Papes

spectacular wooden ceiling was restored in the 1970s.

5 Pope's Chamber

The bedroom here gives a sense of everyday palace life. The pontiffs slept within blue walls decorated with vine and oak-leaf motifs.

6 Stag Room

Clement VI let his extravagant tastes run wild in this study. Frescoes of hunting and fishing in a forest setting cover the walls – the most unusual décor in the palace.

7 Benedict XII's Cloister

These four connecting buildings, surrounding a courtyard, date from 1340. Used for staff and guest accommodation, they were decorated by the Italian artist Simone Martini. They also house the Benedictine chapel.

8 Treasury Halls

The papal wealth was hidden beneath the flagstone floor of the Lower Treasury Hall, while the Upper Treasury Hall functioned as the accounts department.

9 Great Chapel

The Grande Chapelle, with its massive proportions, featured seven vaulted bays and served as the main setting for a variety of religious ceremonies, including papal coronations.

10 Great Audience Hall

This was the meeting place of the popes' formidable judiciary, whose decisions were final and beyond appeal. The ceiling still retains a small section of the *Fresco of the Prophet* – sadly, much of it was stripped away and sold when the palace was used as barracks in the 19th century.

PAPAL AVIGNON

The arrival of the papacy in Avignon *(p130)* brought great prestige to the town. When Pope Gregory XI returned the papacy to Rome in 1377 the French cardinals opposed it. After his death, they elected a French pope, while the Italians chose an Italian one, creating a schism. The row was resolved in 1417 and Avignon popes after Gregory XI are now considered anti-popes.

Clockwise from right **Striking frescoes in the Stag Room; painted ceiling of St John's chapel; ceiling of Palais des Papes; the Pope's Chamber, with its blue walls**

2

GORGES DU VERDON

E3

This vast gorge, carved by the winding waters of the Verdon river, is one of the most spectacular sights in France. Made up of a series of canyons, it stretches for almost 25 km (15 miles) and is up to 700 m (2,300 ft) deep. Its turquoise waters contrast strikingly with the limestone cliffs, creating dramatic scenery at every turn. There's plenty of outdoor activities on offer here, including hiking, kayaking and rafting.

Delightful Moustiers-Sainte-Marie

1 Moustiers-Sainte-Marie

This charming village *(p123)* seems to emerge from the surrounding cliffs, with elegant stone bridges linking houses on either side of the Ravine de Notre-Dame. Known for its earthenware, the village has a small museum and a 12th-century cliffside church, the chapel of Notre-Dame-de-Beauvoir.

EAT

Enjoy fresh seafood and tasty fusion dishes at Le Rhumarin *(saintecroix-lerhumarin.fr)*, while soaking up the lovely lake views from the terrace.

2 Castellane

A pleasant, small town *(p126)*, Castellane is the one of the largest communities in the area and has the widest choice of places to stay and eat. Tour operators here offer a range of activities in the canyon.

3 Lac de Ste-Croix

E3

The hydroelectric dam that created this 10-km- (6-mile-) long lake, south of Moustiers, generates much of Provence's power supply. Electric motorboats, canoes, windsurf boards and catamarans can be hired at Ste-Croix, Les Salles and Bauduen.

4 Aiguines

E3

A stately 17th-century château, with tiled roofs and white turrets, overlooks this attractive village. There are panoramic views over the lake.

5 La Palud-sur-Verdon

La Palud *(p126)* is the base for organized walking expeditions into the canyon, along with adventure activities such as whitewater rafting and kayaking on the rapids.

6 Trigance

F3

This village offers views of the rugged mountain peaks that surround it. It is also a good place to stop for lunch, while taking a tour of the canyon.

Hiking the rugged Blanc-Martel Trail

7 Route des Crêtes

F3

Hiking the Route des Crêtes requires a steady nerve and careful attention to the winding road. Yet it's more than worth it for the breathtaking views over the most dramatic stretches of the canyon.

8 Point Sublime

F3

Close to the village of Rougon, Point Sublime is one of the best places to look down into the rugged landscapes of the gorge. From here, the GR4 trail leads down into the canyon. Be sure to carry a torch to explore the tunnels that cut into the cliffs.

9 La Corniche Sublime

F4

The drive along the Corniche Sublime (D71), on the south side of the canyon, genuinely lives up to its name. Stop at the Balcons de la Mescale for a superb view and marvel at Europe's highest bridge, the Pont de l'Artuby, at 125 m (410 ft) high.

10 Blanc-Martel Trail

Forming part of the much longer GR4 walking trail through the canyon, the Blanc-Martel Trail *(p63)* is the most popular hike through the gorges, passing cliffs and crossing narrow passes.

Cliffs overlooking Lac de Ste-Croix

3

ROMAN ARLES

B4

The charming city of Arles was founded by Greek traders but soon gained favour with Julius Caesar and other later Roman leaders. Built to resemble a miniature version of Rome, Arles spreads out around a massive amphitheatre, with remnants of its Roman heyday – including a theatre and city gates – scattered across the city.

1 Les Arènes

Rond-point des Arènes

This well-preserved arena, built to stage the gladiator contests so loved by the Romans, features two floors of arches and seating for 12,000 spectators. Today, from late April to the end of September, it hosts plays, concerts, sporting events and bullfights.

2 Porte de la Redoute

Two battered gate towers, Porte de la Redoute and Tour des Morgues, flank the Via Aurelia, the highway stretching from Arles to Rome.

EAT

Colosseo Pinsa Romana *(colosseo-pinsa.com)* offers delicious pizzas made with local ingredients, along with stunning views of Les Arènes.

3 Théâtre Antique

Rue du Cloître

All that remains of the Roman theatre, once the cultural heart of Arles, are two elegant columns, also known as the "two widows". Though much of the original structure has disappeared over time, these remnants offer a quiet glimpse into the city's Roman past and the role this theatre once played in daily life.

4 Église St-Trophime

This spectacular Romanesque church *(p47)*, with its beautiful carved stonework, was originally devoted to St Stephen. In the 11th century, however, it became the church of St Trophimus.

Clockwise from right **Lion sculpture at the Egyptian Obelisk; arched gallery at Cryptoportiques du Forum; historic Théâtre Antique; busy market at place du Forum**

5 Egyptian Obelisk

Pl de la République

Adorned with sculpted lions at its base, this square-sided obelisk is believed to have been brought to Arles as a trophy following Rome's conquest of Egypt during the reign of Augustus.

6 Cryptoportiques du Forum

Pl de la Republique

This amazing labyrinth of chambers beneath the ancient Forum was the city's granary, carved out of the ground during the 1st century BCE.

7 Place du Forum

Although nothing remains of the original Roman Forum – the bustling market that once formed the heart of Arles – its legacy lives on. Today, the place du Forum still serves as a lively gathering spot.

Exterior of the arena at Roman Arles

8 Les Thermes de Constantin

Rue du Grand Prieuré

A semicircular apse marks the site of the once-palatial bathhouse built in the 4th century CE, in the reign of Emperor Constantine.

9 Les Alyscamps

Av des Alyscamps

This long avenue of marble sarcophagi marks the site of the Roman necropolis where the city's dignitaries were buried. It is also claimed that Christ appeared here at the burial of St Trophimus, the first bishop of Arles.

10 Musée Départemental Arles Antique

Av de la 1ère Division Française Libre

This museum has the finest collection of Roman sculptures in Provence, including a statue of Venus and the impressive Altar of Apollo. Also on display is a well-preserved Roman barge, recovered from the bed of the Rhône.

AIX-EN-PROVENCE

C4 300 Av Giuseppe Verdi; aixenprovencetourism.com

Aix-en-Provence is a sophisticated city, whether in the dignified squares and little streets of the Old Quarter or amid the elegant townhouses and tree-lined avenues of the 17th- and 18th-century district. The city is also a lively place thanks to its international student population, who come to study at one of the country's oldest universities.

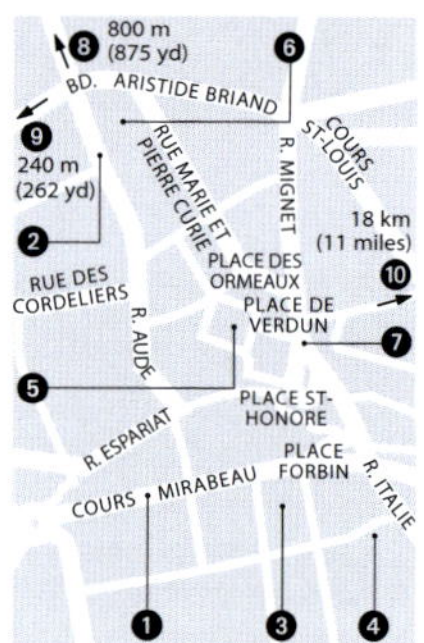

1 Cours Mirabeau

Created in 1650, Aix's majestic main avenue, cours Mirabeau, features giant plane trees, which form a stunning canopy over the tall townhouses. Lively cafés line its northern side, while a series of fountains adds freshness to the grandeur.

2 Rue Gaston-de-Saporta

Running from the town hall to the cathedral, this is the liveliest thoroughfare of the Old Quarter, buzzing with commerce.

3 Quartier Mazarin

Aix nobility built some of their finest townhouses in this area in the 17th and 18th centuries. Within this tranquil district of ornamental façades, small galleries and antiques shops, the discreet air of old money remains palpable.

4 Musée Granet

Pl St-Jean-de-Malte Hours vary, check website museegranet-aixenprovence.fr

Housed in a former priory, this museum, built in 1671, displays European art from the 16th to 19th centuries.

5 Granet XXe

Pl Jean-Boyer Hours vary, check website museegranet-aixenprovence.fr

The 16th-century Chapelle des Pénitents Blancs, an outpost of the Musée Granet, hosts artworks belonging to Swiss collector Jean Planque. It showcases over 300 works by artists such as Renoir, Monet, Van Gogh and Picasso.

6 Cathédrale St-Sauveur

34 pl des Martyrs de la Résistance 8am–6pm daily paroisses-aixarles.fr/aix-saintsauveur

This is the focal point of medieval Aix. Notable

Cathédrale St-Sauveur

Exploring the busy Cours Mirabeau

features include an octagonal, 5th-century baptistry, 12th-century carved cloisters and the wonderful *Buisson Ardent (Burning Bush)* triptych painted in 1476 by Nicolas Froment.

7 Aix Market

Pl de l'Hôtel de Ville

The vast and colourful Aix market is spread across the city's old squares on Tuesday, Thursday and Saturday mornings. From the place de Verdun via the place des Prêcheurs to the place de l'Hôtel de Ville, the streets come alive with stalls selling fresh produce, clothes and antiques.

Fresh produce on sale at Aix market

8 Atelier de Cézanne

Av Paul Cézanne
Hours vary, check website
cezanne-en-provence.com

Paul Cézanne's studio, from 1902 until his death, has been left as it was – a jumble of artist's tools, furniture and still-life subjects.

9 Pavillon de Vendôme

32 rue Célony
10am–12:30pm & 1:30–5pm Wed–Mon (mid-Apr–mid-Oct: to 6pm Wed–Mon)
Jan
aixenprovence.fr

Obliged to enter holy orders, local cardinal Louis de Mercoeur built this villa as a love-nest for his mistress in 1665. Its size, intricate façade and extensive gardens, however, suggest a somewhat open secret. The pavilion now houses several contemporary art exhibitions.

EAT

The city's most famous sweet treats are *calissons d'Aix* *(p68)*. Visit Le Roy Rene *(calisson.com/fr)* to sample these almond-and-melon biscuits.

10 Mont Sainte-Victoire

D4

East of Aix, at 1,000 m (3,300 ft) high and 7 km (11 miles) across, this mountain exerts an almost mystical power over the region. Cézanne *(p50)* was so fascinated by its changing moods that he painted it more than 60 times. On its northern slopes is the Château de Vauvenargues, former home and burial place of Picasso *(p51)*.

VIEUX NICE

Q4–5 5 promenade des Anglais explorenicecotedazur.com

A maze of narrow streets lined with stunning Baroque architecture, Nice's Old Town brims with life. Here, lively markets offer everything from fresh flowers to seafood; food stalls fill the air with irresistible aromas; and the terraces of the pastel-hued buildings house bars and restaurants, where locals come to kick back in the evenings.

1 Cathédrale Ste-Réparate

Pl Rossetti
Hours vary, check website cathedrale-nice.fr

During the rule of the Dukes of Savoy, this grand 17th-century church was Nice's main place of worship. It features a stunning polychrome cupola and, inside, breathtaking Baroque stucco décor.

2 Cours Saleya

This large, oblong square is a bustling spot throughout the week. On Monday mornings it plays host to an antiques and flea market, while every other morning it is the location of the city's world-famous flower market, where you can pick up colourful and sweet-smelling bouquets. Come evening, the bar and restaurant terraces around the square buzz with activity.

TOP TIP

Parking is available at place Masséna, as Vieux Nice is a pedestrian-only area.

3 Rue St-François-de-Paule

This street is home to two of the city's most beloved institutions: Maison Auer, a delightful *chocolaterie*, at No 7; and Alziari, renowned for its olives and "grand cru", at No 14.

4 Rue Pairolière

This narrow street is lined with food stalls that overflow with *socca* (chickpea pancakes),

Distinctive Cathédrale Ste-Réparate

TRANSPORT The easiest way to reach Colline du Château is to take the lift from quai des États-Unis. Alternatively, there's a staircase.

salt cod and spicy meats. Other stalls here sell items such as Provençal fabrics and jewellery.

5 Place St-François

Dominated by an 18th-century clock tower and a Baroque palace, this square hosts a fish and herb market around its dolphin fountain.

6 Palais Lascaris

15 rue Droite
10am–6pm Wed–Mon nice.fr/lieux/palais-lascaris

This 17th-century Baroque palace now houses a museum dedicated to historic musical instruments.

7 Opéra de Nice

4–6 rue St-François-de-Paule
opera-nice.org

This ornate building is home to ballet, classical music and opera performances. Designed by François Aune, a pupil of Gustave Eiffel, the theatre was rebuilt in 1885, after a fire destroyed the original structure. It was later classified as a historic monument in 1993.

8 Chapelle de la Miséricorde

Cours Saleya
2:30–5:30pm Tue

If you visit just one Baroque church in Nice, make it this one. Its decoration makes it one of the finest examples of Baroque architecture in the world.

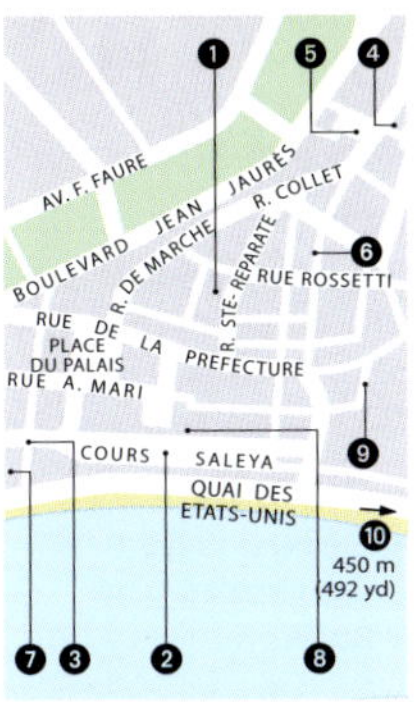

9 Quartier du Malonat

In the quaint Quartier du Malonat, everyday life unfolds quietly in its narrow streets and small squares. The sight of laundry hanging from windows adds a touch of the ordinary, while the *trompe l'oeil* paintings on the buildings bring a subtle charm to the area.

10 Colline du Château

Once home to a castle destroyed in 1706, the hilltop Colline du Château offers stunning views over both Nice and the twinkling sea beyond. At its base is a leafy botanical garden, which provides a tranquil escape from the city's hustle and bustle.

Beautiful staircase in Palais Lascaris

ST-TROPEZ

F5 Quai Jean Jaurès; sainttropeztourisme.com

St-Tropez conjures up images of glamorous beach life, celebrity yachts and upmarket shopping, but there's more to the town than just luxury. The ochre-painted walls and terracotta rooftops of La Ponche evoke a time before tourism, while the works on display in the Musée de l'Annonciade highlight the town's role as a muse for many great artists.

1 Notre-Dame-de-l'Assomption

Rue Commandant Guichard 9:30am–noon daily

This ebullient Italian Baroque church, built in the early 1800s, has a gilded bust of the town's patron saint, Tropez (or Torpès). According to legend, the Roman legionary converted to Christianity and was martyred by Emperor Nero. His body was pushed out to sea by the Romans before washing up where the town now stands.

2 Vieux Port

The quayside of the Old Port, quai Jean Jaurès, is lined with leisure vessels year-round. In summer, it buzzes with artists, and pedestrians hoping to spot a celeb.

3 Musée de l'Annonciade

Close to the Vieux Port, this pretty 16th-century chapel has been converted to house into a world-class art museum *(p48)*. Its collection focuses on paintings by famous artists connected with St-Tropez, including Bonnard, Derain, Dufy, Matisse, Rouault and Signac. Note, some parts of the museum may be closed for renovation between 2026 and 2028.

DRINK

Le Café on place des Lices is where artists hung out in the 1950s and 1960s heyday. It is an institution now, but little has changed.

4 Place des Lices

Immortalized by the painter Charles Camoin, this charming market square is shaded by plane trees and filled with open-air café tables. It is the perfect spot to watch locals playing *pétanque* (boules). On Tuesday and Saturday mornings, the square transforms into a vibrant market with stalls selling antiques, flowers and fruit.

5 Citadel

⌂ Mnt de la Citadelle

Built to protect the village from Barbary corsairs, this fort features 17th-century ramparts. It houses the Musée d'Histoire Maritime, which traces the area's maritime history and highlights the lives of notable residents, like Pierre-André de Suffren, a prominent admiral during France's 18th-century wars with Britain.

6 Tour Suffren

⌂ Pl Raphaël de Garrezio

Built in 880 CE by Guillaume I, Duke of Provence, this tower overlooking the harbour, where old boats are moored, was once part of the Château Suffren.

7 La Ponche

La Ponche is the core of the original fishing village. With narrow streets, painted shutters and ochre walls, it looks much as it did before tourism arrived.

8 La Fontanette

⌂ Rue Fontannette

Just east of La Ponche, La Fontanette beach is set within walking distance of the town. It's an ideal place to enjoy a swim while exploring St-Tropez.

9 Sentier des Douaniers

⌂ D98–D559

The "Customs Officers' Path" is part of a longer coastal path which provides views of the Côte d'Azur. The bays offer bathing opportunities away from the crowds. Energetic walkers can follow the path for 35 km (21 miles) to Cavalaire.

10 Plage de Pampelonne

St-Tropez's beaches *(p58)* begin 4 km (2.5 miles) southeast of the town, on a long bay, the Anse de Pampelonne. The 5-km (3-mile) sweep of sand is divided into smaller stretches, each with its own name.

ARTISTIC HUB

St-Tropez transformed from a remote fishing village to a holiday spot thanks to painter Paul Signac *(p50)*. He arrived in 1887, fell in love with the light and colour and chose to stay. More painters, writers and would-be artists followed, drawn by the warm weather and easy life. The film industry found the scene in the 1950s, and later, so did the jet set. Brigitte Bardot became its icon in the Swinging Sixties and St-Tropez has never looked back.

The colourful houses of La Ponche

7

THE CAMARGUE

A4–B5

Black bulls, wild white horses and pink flamingos: these are the classic images of the Camargue delta, where the mighty Rhône meets the Mediterranean. It's a 1,000-sq-km (386-sq-mile) zone of lagoons, salt flats and marshes, remote, romantic and rich in birdlife. Large stretches are protected and inaccessible, but open to all are the beautiful views of nature and stunning sunsets.

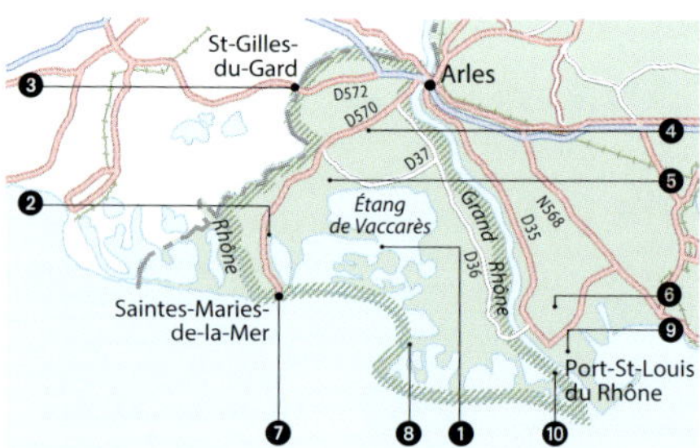

1 Parc Naturel Régional de Camargue

La Capelière
04 90 97 00 97

The HQ of this reserve has displays on ecosystems and climate. Nature trails and observation posts test your new knowledge.

2 Parc Ornithologique du Pont-de-Gau

Near the information centre, this bird park *(p90)* features aviaries dotted around 1 ha (2 acres) of marshland, home to rare birds that are difficult to spot in the wild.

3 Abbaye de St-Gilles

Pl de la République

This once-vast medieval abbey, in St-Gilles-du-Gard, was severely damaged in 1562. The elaborately carved façade of the building, one of Provence's most beautiful, has survived and remains intact today.

4 Musée de la Camargue

A converted sheep barn *(p90)* is a fine setting for a little museum dealing with the interaction of humans and nature in the Camargue, from the 19th century to the present day.

Wild horses in the Camargue

EAT

Book a barbecue lunch at a *manade* (farm), such as La Table de la Manade *(masdes jasses.com)*. It offers tasty Camargue bull steaks.

5 Domaine de Méjanes

W mejanes-camargue.fr

The peaceful banks of Vaccarès lagoon are a good place to spy Camargue white horses and flamingos.

6 Saltpans

A4–B4

The largest saltpans in Europe, located in the southeast of the Camargue region, cover 100 sq km (40 sq miles) and produce an impressive 800,000 tonnes of salt a year. Visitors can easily reach the great mounds of salt by boarding a train at Salin d'Aigues Mortes *(04 66 73 40 24)*.

7 Saintes-Maries-de-la-Mer

D570

The tiny main street of this old village teems with crowds in summer, but its seaside charm remains intact. The May pilgrimage of the Romani people marks the legendary arrival of Mary Magdalene, Mary Jacoby, Mary Salome and their servant Sara, who is the patron saint of Romani peoples.

8 Plage de Beauduc

B5

The "beach at the end of the world" is the spot for wild camping and watersports in summer. Vehicles are not permitted here.

9 Port-St-Louis-du-Rhône

B5 **Tour St Louis, quai Bonnardel; port saintlouistourisme.fr**

This port town has an 18th-century tower, which served as a lookout post. The tower now houses an ornithological museum and offers superb views of the salt marshes.

CAMARGUE BIRDLIFE

The Camargue is a paradise for bird-watchers, particularly in spring when migrant birds visit on their journey north. The iconic flamingoes stalk the delta's shallow lagoons, but there are other birds as well. This is the only French breeding site of the slender-billed gull; the red-crested pochard also breeds here.

10 Domaine de la Palissade

B5 Salin de Giraud

W palissade.fr

Visitors can explore the rich flora and fauna of this natural reserve either on foot (walks range in duration from 30 minutes to 3 hours 30 minutes) or, from April to October, in the saddle on a Camargue horse.

Pink and orange hues across the saltpans

VAISON-LA-ROMAINE

C2 Pl du Chanoine Sautel; vaison-ventoux-provence.com

Straddling a steep-sided gorge on the river Ouvèze, Vaison-la-Romaine is a picturesque town, home to a vast and well-preserved Roman archaeological site. There's also a beautiful medieval old town, Haute Ville, which is linked to the Roman area via the graceful, single-arched Pont Romain.

Ruins of the archaeological site in Puymin

1 Puymin

Pl du Chanoine Sautel

Named for the hill on which it stands, this district was the most important part of the old Roman town, home to the *praetorium* (courthouse), a theatre, temples and shops. There are also many well-preserved houses here.

2 Maison des Messii

The House of the Messii was probably home to one of the Roman town's most important families. Columns and foundations of an atrium, baths, a dining room and living rooms, as well as a temple to household gods, can all still be seen.

3 House with the Silver Bust

Named after a statue found here (and now on show in the Musée Théo Desplans), the ruins of this once grand, mosaic-floored villa are enhanced by copies of statues found here and elsewhere on the archaeological site.

4 House with the Dolphin

The House with the Dolphin was named after a marble statue of Cupid riding a dolphin that was found here, now on display in the Musée Théo Desplans. The villa once had a façade supported by 18 columns.

5 Musée Théo Desplans

Pl du Chanoine Sautel
Hours vary, check website provenceromaine.com

A life-size marble nude of the Emperor Hadrian, a statue of his empress Sabina and a six-seater public latrine are among the more interesting archaeological finds in this excellent museum, found within the archaeological area.

6 Portico of Pompey

This impressive portico, built around 20 CE by the

The impressive interior of the Théâtre Antique

Vaison-la-Romaine, overlooking the river Ouvèze

family of Caesar's great rival Pompey, is a huge, 65-m (210-ft) array of columns, which originally surrounded an inner garden. Copies of statues that once stood on the site now grace the niches – the originals are in the Musée Théo Desplans.

7 Théâtre Antique

Rue Bernard Noël

This 1st-century CE theatre is a display of Roman building skill, with 34 semicircular rows of stone benches, seating up to 7,000 spectators, rising to a columned portico.

8 Nymphaeum

Rue Sabine

The Nymphaeum was a rectangular sacred pool with a fountain, which was covered by a roof supported by four columns. Traces of the building still remain, as does the sacred spring which provided the water supply. It now forms an elegant backdrop to an open-air theatre.

9 Pont Romain and Haute Ville

Grande Rue

Vaison's 2,000-year-old Roman bridge connects the archaeological area on the north side of the Ouvèze with the Haute Ville on the south bank. Ringed by ramparts and entered through a 14th-century stone gateway, this area is home to 17th-century townhouses, courtyards and fountains.

TOP TIP

Comfy shoes, sun hat and sunscreen, and a water bottle are a must – especially in summer.

10 Château

Montée du Château

At the highest point of the Haute Ville stands a dramatic, part-ruined castle, built in 1160 by the Count of Toulouse. Three main wings and a keep tower surround an inner courtyard.

ABBAYE NOTRE-DAME DE SÉNANQUE

C3 84220 Gordes 10–11am & 1–5pm Mon–Sat, 1–5pm Sun Mid-Nov–Jan (am), Ascension (sixth Sun after Easter), 15 Aug, 1 Nov, snow days senanque.fr

Swathes of purple lavender surround this serene 12th-century Cistercian abbey, founded in 1148 by an abbot and 12 monks. While later centuries saw the monastery face attack, plague and anti-monastic laws, it survived, and today is home to a small community of monks who dedicate their lives to prayer and to maintaining the abbey and its land.

1 Apse

The three windows of the raised, semicircular apse in the abbey symbolize the Holy Trinity.

2 Nave and Transept

The barrel-vaulted nave and aisles of Sénanque are five bays long. Stone steps lead from the nave to the square crossing, with its eight-sided dome.

3 Cloister

The dove-grey limestone columns of the cloister, decorated with delicate carvings of leaves, flowers and vines, are superb works of craftsmanship, dating from 1180 to 1220.

4 Abbey Shop

The Cistercians believe in work as well as prayer, and the fruits of their labours are here. This shop sells their own lavender essential oil and honey from their hives, and books and products made in other convents and monasteries across France.

5 Channels

The Cistercians came to this plateau seeking isolation, and built their abbey next

to the region's only river, the Senancole. They channelled the water to flow through and under the abbey, providing sanitation and irrigation for the gardens.

6 Calefactory

The calefactory and scriptorium reflects St Bernard's injunctions against luxury: with two fireplaces, this was the only heated room in the monastery, allowing the monks to read without their hands freezing.

7 Dormitory

The dormitory is a huge, vaulted space, paved with flagstones. Arched windows placed at regular intervals along its walls and two large, circular windows at each end make this otherwise austere room feel pleasantly light and airy.

8 Tomb of the Seigneur de Venasque

In one corner of the east arm of the transept is the only non-Cistercian element of the church – a Gothic tomb, which marks the burial place of Geoffroy, the 13th-century Lord of Venasque and, at one time, the abbey's benefactor.

9 Lavender Fields

The abbey of Notre-Dame de Sénanque is surrounded by lavender fields, which make a spectacular setting for the buildings in the summer.

10 Chapterhouse

The walls of the square chapterhouse are lined with stone seats. Here the monks sat to listen to a chapter from the Rule of St Benedict or a sermon from the Bible.

ST BERNARD AND THE CISTERCIANS

With their complete lack of decoration or comfort, Provence's most outstanding Romanesque monasteries, Sénanque, Silvacane *(p88)* and Le Thoronet *(p94)*, reflect the austere ideals of the Cistercian order, founded in 1098 by St Bernard, abbot of Clairvaux in northeast France. Rejecting the ostentation and luxury of the powerful Benedictine order, St Bernard advocated a rigorous and pure monastic life within simple, graceful and harmonious buildings.

The abbey, enclosed by lavender fields

ST-PAUL-DE-VENCE

G4 Office du Tourisme: 2 rue Grande; open 10am–6pm Mon–Fri, 10am–1pm & 2–6pm Sat; saint-pauldevence.com

Set in Alpine hinterland with panoramic views of the Riviera coast, the beautifully sited St-Paul-de-Vence first drew painters in the 1920s. The village's maze of medieval streets, full of modern art galleries and workshops, is a delight to stroll through, with a must-visit being the outstanding art collection of the Fondation Maeght.

Medieval village of St-Paul-de-Vence

1 Les Remparts

Visitors can walk around the village's unspoilt 16th-century ramparts – originally built to resist assault from Piedmont and Savoy – and enjoy a panoramic view of the vineyards and olive groves that cloak the hilly countryside.

ARTISTS IN ST-PAUL-DE-VENCE

Drawn to the colours, light and views of the coast, artists like Paul Signac and Raoul Dufy were the first to visit St-Paul-de-Vence, followed by others such as Matisse and Picasso. Poet Jacques Prévert lived here for 15 years, while writer James Baldwin spent his last days in the village.

2 Église Collégiale

Pl de l'Église
8:15am–4:15pm Mon–Fri, 10am–6pm Sat, Sun & public hols

Built between the 14th and the 18th centuries, this small church's highlight is the 1680 Chapelle Saint Clément, decorated in ornate Baroque style.

3 Chapelle St Charles-St Claude

Nestled on a promontory above the village's ramparts, this chapel was set up in the 17th century. In the early 2010s, Nice artist Paul Conte painted it with colourful murals depicting scenes from the lives of its patron saints.

4 Fondation Maeght

Home to one of Europe's largest collections of 20th-century art, Fondation Maeght *(p48)* was set up by Cannes art dealers Aimé and Marguerite Maeght. Their private art collection formed the basis of the foundation.

5 La Chapelle Folon (Chapelle des Pénitents Blancs)

Pl de l'Église
Hours vary, check website Nov, 25 Dec, 1 Jan

Artist Jean-Michel Folon collaborated with local artisans to decorate this 17th-century chapel with stained-glass windows, sculptures, murals and mosaics. The chapel is immaculately preserved as a celebration of him.

Cobblestoned rue Grande lined with cafés

EAT
Dine at the popular La Colombe d' Or *(la-colombe-dor.com)* on place du Général de Gaulle, a 1920s inn adorned with paintings by renowned artists.

6 Place de Gaulle

Locals meet at this square, also known as place du Jeu de Boules, for a friendly game of *pétanque* under the plane trees. Contests usually take place during summer.

7 Cimetière

Chem de Nice

Marc Chagall *(p51)*, who lived in St-Paul-de-Vence for almost 20 years, is the most famous resident of the village's cemetery. His modest, cedar-shaded grave is a place of pilgrimage for admirers, who leave small stones in a growing pile as visible tributes.

8 Place de la Grande Fontaine

Built in 1615, the pretty fountain in place de la Grande Fontaine is of typical Provençal design. A favourite subject for artists, it is one of the village's most photographed sights. The square where it stands also hosted a weekly market in the Middle Ages.

9 Donjon (Tour de la Mairie)

Once part of the village's now-demolished château, this keep was one of the first stuctures to be built here. Its bell tower dates back to the 1440s. Today, it houses the town hall.

Fountain at the place de la Grande Fontaine

10 Rue Grande

St-Paul's main thoroughfare, rue Grande is lined with studios and workshops of local artists and artisans. The street is a veritable open-air art museum, with the latest works of local talents displayed in the windows of fashionable commercial galleries.

TOP 10 OF EVERYTHING

Frescoes in Notre-Dame des Fontaines, La Brigue

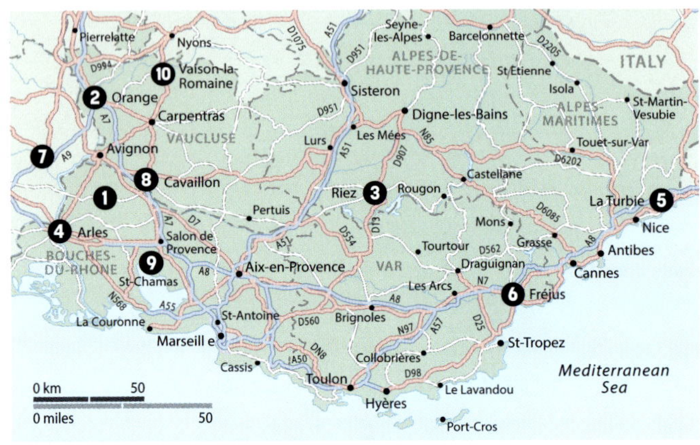

ROMAN SIGHTS

1 Les Antiques de Glanum

B3 Av Vincent Van Gogh, 13210 St-Rémy Daily site-glanum.fr

Twin temples, a Roman forum, baths and a fortified gate can be seen at Glanum, near St-Rémy *(p89)*, which also has traces of a 4th-century BCE Greek settlement. A triumphal arch (10 BCE) marks Gallic victories.

2 Théâtre Antique d'Orange, Vaucluse

Built during the reign of Augustus (c 27–25 BCE), this is one of the best-preserved theatres of the Roman empire *(p129)* and a highlight of the Parc de la Colline St-Eutrope. A triumphal arch decorated with relief carvings commemorates Julius Caesar's victories over Gaul.

The Théâtre Antique d'Orange in Vaucluse

3 Temple of Apollo, Riez

E3

Just outside Riez on the Valensole plateau, four Corinthian columns of the 1st-century-CE temple to Apollo are all that remain of the once-prosperous Roman settlement of Reia Apollinaris. Eight ancient pillars, perhaps scavenged from another Roman building, are now in the early Christian church nearby, which dates from the 4th or 5th century CE and is one of the oldest surviving churches in France.

4 Arles

Remnants of Provence's most important Roman settlement *(p26)* can still be seen in numerous spots around this lovely city.

5 La Trophée d'Auguste, La Turbie

This Roman monument *(p117)*, built from local white stone, was erected in 6 BCE to mark the boundary between Italy and

La Trophée d'Auguste towering over La Turbie

Gaul and to honour Augustus's Gallic conquests. Towering over the village of La Turbie, high above Monte Carlo, it offers breathtaking views over the Riviera.

6 Les Arènes de Fréjus

F4 Rue H Vadon Apr–Sep: 9:30am–12:30pm & 2–6pm Tue–Sun; Oct–Mar: 9:30am–noon & 2–4:30pm Tue–Sat Public hols ville-frejus.fr

Like other large Roman arenas in Provence, the amphitheatre at Fréjus *(p93)* can seat up to 10,000 people. Built in the 1st and 2nd centuries CE, it is still regularly used for bullfights and classical music concerts. Nearby are parts of the original Roman wall.

7 Pont du Gard

A3

The Romans considered this 49-m- (160-ft-) high three-tiered bridge to be clear testimony to their empire's greatness. The top tier was part of an aqueduct that supplied Nîmes with water for up to 500 years. Constructed in the 1st century CE from dressed stone blocks without mortar, the bridge is 275 m (900 ft) long and represents an astonishing feat of engineering.

8 Arc de Triomphe, Cavaillon

C3

Constructed in the 1st century CE, during the reign of the Emperor Augustus, this twin-arched triumphal gate is adorned with carved veins and Corinthian columns. The town's archaeological museum houses other fascinating Roman artifacts.

9 Pont Flavien, St-Chamas

One of the best-preserved Roman bridges in France, Pont Flavien *(p90)* was built over the River Touloubre in the 1st century CE. Constructed as part of Emperor Augustus's Via Julia Augusta, which linked Piacenzia (Palantia) in Italy to Arles, it is the only bridge bookended by triumphal arches to have survived.

10 Vaison-la-Romaine

Early 20th-century excavations in Vaison-la-Romaine *(p36)* uncovered numerous Roman sites, as well as artifacts, some dating back to the late Neolithic period (c 7000–3000 BCE). Spread across 15 ha (37 acres), the area is now a vast, open-air archaeological complex accessible to the public.

Well-preserved Pont du Gard, a Roman aqueduct bridge

PLACES OF WORSHIP

1 Chapelle des Pénitents Blancs, Les Baux-de-Provence

B4 10am–5pm daily (Apr–Sep: to 7pm)

This chapel's 1974 frescoes by local artist Yves Brayer depict a typical Provençal nativity scene with shepherds. More of Brayer's work can be seen at the nearby Musée Yves Brayer *(yvesbrayer.com)*.

2 Notre-Dame-du-Puy, Grasse

G4 8 pl du Petit Puy Oct–Mar: 9am–noon & 2–5pm Mon–Sat; Apr–Sep: 9am–noon & 2–5pm Mon, 10am–noon & 1–6pm Tue–Sat

Fragonard's *Christ Washing the Disciples' Feet* is the main reason for visiting this 13th-century church. It also contains three magnificent religious works by Rubens, all painted in 1601: *The Crown of Thorns*, *The Crucifixion of Christ* and *The Deposition of St Helena*.

3 Notre-Dame des Fontaines, La Brigue

H2 Rue Notre-Dame des Fontaines Mid-Apr–Sep: 10am–12:30pm & 2–5:30pm Fri–Wed Thu

This chapel, 4 km (2.5 miles) from La Brigue *(p120)*, is covered with remarkable frescoes by Giovanni Canavesio and Giovanni Baleison, dating from 1492.

4 Notre-Dame-de-Nazareth, Vaison-la-Romaine

C2 Rue Alphonse Daudet 04 90 36 05 65 Jun–Sep: 9am–6pm daily

This evocative 6th-century cathedral has a superb arcaded apse and 12th-century cloister.

5 Abbaye de Montmajour

The abbey of Montmajour *(p87)* was built on a rocky island amid the Rhône marshes. It was an important pilgrimage site and became wealthy from selling pardons for sins. The cloister is decorated with mythical and biblical scenes.

6 Cathédrale St-Léonce, Fréjus

F4 Pl Camille Formigé 7am–7pm daily; cloisters: Jan–Apr & Sep–Dec: 10am–1pm & 2–5pm Tue–Sun; May–Aug: 10am–6pm daily 1 Jan, 1 May, 1 & 11 Nov, 25 Dec

Constructed in the pink stone typical of Fréjus *(p93)*, this 13th-century cathedral has a beautiful Renaissance doorway. Its interior is dominated by pointed arches, and the cloister ceiling, with its scenes of the Apocalypse, is unique. Note, there's an admission fee to visit the cloisters.

Frescoes at Notre-Dame des Fontaines

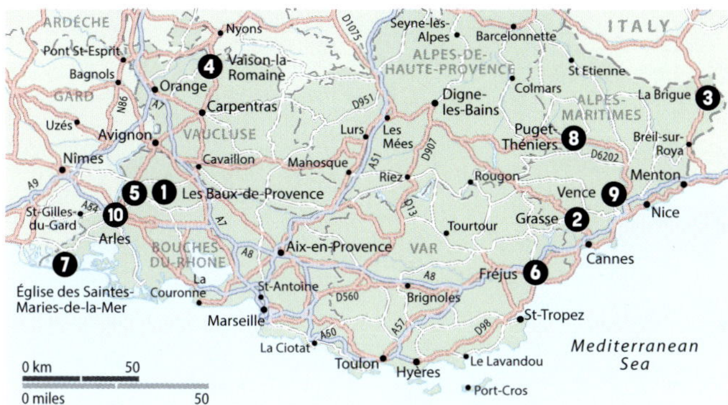

7 Église des Saintes-Maries-de-la-Mer

The bell tower of this fortified church *(p90)* is a Camargue landmark. The church has lent its name to the capital of the region, and its sturdy walls offered refuge from raiders. The most colourful sight within is a carved boat with statues of the Virgin and Mary Magdalene and a statue of St Sara in the crypt. The Romani pilgrimage in May *(p35)* marks the legendary arrival of Mary Magdalene by boat.

8 Notre-Dame-de-l'Assomption, Puget-Théniers

G3 Pl de l'Eglise 8am–6pm daily

Built by the Knights Templar, the 13th-century parish church of this mountain village *(p120)* has a lovely triptych altarpiece, *Notre-Dame-de-Bon-Secours*, which depicts the Passion, painted by Antoine Ronzen in 1525. The group of wooden sculptures has been attributed to the sculptor Matthieu d'Anvers or Flemish or Burgundian craftspeople.

9 Chapelle du Rosaire de Vence

G4 466 av Henri Matisse 10am–noon & 2–5pm Tue, Thu, Fri (Mar–Oct: to 6pm), 2–5pm Wed & Sat (Mar–Oct: to 6pm); Mass: 10am Sun 1st two weeks Dec, public hols

The dazzling white interior walls of this little chapel are adorned with black line drawings of the Stations of the Cross. They are the work of Henri Matisse *(p50)*, who designed this building in 1949.

10 Église St-Trophime, Arles

B4 6 pl de la République May–Sep: 9am–7pm daily; Mar, Apr, Oct 9am–6pm daily; Nov–Feb: 10:30am–4:30pm daily

Dating to 450 CE, this is one of the region's most beautiful churches. It was rebuilt in the 11th century and dedicated to St Trophimus. Note, there's an entry fee to visit the cloisters.

Façade of the Église St-Trophime in Arles

ART GALLERIES

1 Musée National Marc Chagall, Nice

Q3 Av du Dr Ménard Hours vary, check website musees-nationaux-alpesmaritimes.fr/chagall

One of the jewels of Provence, this museum houses the world's largest collection of works by Marc Chagall, including 17 canvases from his *Biblical Message* series.

2 Musée Fernand Léger, Biot

Q3 Chemin du Val-de-Pôme Hours vary, check website musees-nationaux-alpes maritimes.fr/flege

Mosaics in primary colours, carried out to Léger's own design, identify this strikingly modern museum. The Cubist painter planned to build a studio here just before his death in 1955, and the museum exhibits more than 400 of his works.

3 Fondation Maeght, St-Paul-de-Vence

G4 623 chemin des Gardettes 04 93 32 81 63 Hours vary, call ahead

This small museum has an array of modern art, including paintings by Léger, Bonnard and Chagall, sculpture by Miró and a mosaic pool by Braque.

4 Musée Renoir, Cagnes-sur-Mer

Auguste Renoir's house *(p109)* at Les Collettes, where the painter hoped that the climate would cure his rheumatism, houses 11 of his paintings. The house is surrounded by beautiful olive groves.

5 Musée Picasso, Antibes

Housed in the Château Grimaldi, used as a studio by Picasso in 1946, the museum *(p108)* contains around 250 of his paintings, sketches and ceramics, as well as works by Léger and Miró.

6 Musée de l'Annonciade, St-Tropez

Q3 Pl Georges Grammont Hours vary, check website saint-tropez.fr/culture/musee-de-lannonciad

Opened in 1955, this former chapel houses an art collection *(p32)*. It has works by Pierre Bonnard, Paul Signac and Charles Camoin, whose *St-Tropez, la place des Lices et le Café des Arts* (1925) is a famous depiction of the town.

7 Musée Bonnard, Le Cannet

G4 16 blvd Sadi Carnot 10am–6pm Tue–Sun (Jul & Aug: to 8pm daily)

Pierre Bonnard spent most of 1926–47 in Le Cannet, and this museum in a belle

Auguste Renoir's studio at Musée Renoir

époque villa, displays some of his finest canvases. Links with the Musée d'Orsay in Paris bring frequent special exhibitions.

8 Musée d'Art Moderne et d'Art Contemporain (MAMAC), Nice

A striking example of contemporary architecture, this museum *(p101)* features marble-faced towers and glass corridors and contains works by some of the 20th century's greatest avant-garde artists.

9 Musée Jean Cocteau, Menton

H3 Quai Napoléon III 10am–12:30pm & 2–6pm Wed–Mon musee cocteaumenton.fr

Famous poet, playwright and filmmaker, Jean Cocteau (1889–1963) converted Le Bastion, a 17th-century fort, into his personal museum. Nearby, the Collection Séverin Wunderman *(temporarily closed for renovation)* has 1,800 pieces of art donated by the eponymous art enthusiast and admirer of Cocteau.

10 Musée Matisse, Nice

Founded in 1963, nine years after the painter's death, the Musée Matisse *(p101)* is located in the 17th-century Villa des Arènes. It showcases sketches, paintings, bronze sculptures and some of his personal effects.

Villa des Arènes, the setting for the Musée Matisse

TOP 10 MASTERPIECES OF PROVENCE

***L'Orage* by Paul Signac**

1. L'Orage
Pointillist Paul Signac's 1895 work in the Musée de l'Annonciade depicts St-Tropez harbour.

2. Wagons de Chemin de Fer à Arles
Painted in 1888 by Van Gogh, this work is set in the Musée Angladon *(p132)*.

3. La Joie de Vivre
One of Picasso's best works, this 1946 piece is in the Musée Picasso, Antibes.

4. La Partie de Campagne
Fernand Léger's painting is on display at the Fondation Maeght.

5. Nu Bleu IV
This 1952 work in the Musée Matisse is among the best known of the artist's blue paper cut-outs.

6. Coronation of the Virgin
Enguerrand Quarton's 1453 altarpiece painting can be seen in the Musée Pierre de Luxembourg.

7. Venus Victrix
One of Renoir's magnificent bronzes (1914) can be found at Les Collettes.

8. Les Baigneuses
Cézanne painted a smaller scene of *The Bathers* around 1895. It is on display at the Musée Granet *(p28)*.

9. The Burning Bush
Nicolas Froment's 1476 triptych in the Cathédrale St-Sauveur *(p28)* was commissioned by Provence's king, René.

10. La Terrasse à l'Estaque
This early Cubist work (1908) in the Musée Cantini *(p83)* is part of a trio Raoul Dufy painted of the village.

PAINTERS IN PROVENCE

1 Paul Guigou

Realist painter Paul Guigou (1834–71) illustrated the landscapes of his native Vaucluse. Among his best-known works is *Deux Lavandières devant la Sainte-Victoire*, in the Musée Grobet-Labadié *(p83)* in Marseille.

2 Paul Cézanne

Born in Aix, where he lived most of his life, Cézanne (1839–1906) painted hundreds of oil and watercolour scenes of his home city and the nearby Mont Sainte-Victoire *(p29)* in his Post-Impressionist style. He captured the soul of Provence better than any painter.

3 Vincent van Gogh

The Dutch Post-Impressionist created hundreds of his most vivid, powerful landscapes and self-portraits during his few years in Arles *(p26)* and St-Rémy *(p89)*. The sunshine of Provence is said to have changed the way Van Gogh (1853–90) saw light and colour.

4 Paul Signac

A master of the Pointillist style, Signac (1863–1935) came to St-Tropez *(p32)* in 1892. He found, in the sparkle of sun on sea, the perfect subject for Pointillism's technique of using a myriad of tiny rainbow dots to depict swathes or blocks of colour.

5 Henri Matisse

Matisse (1869–1954) lived in Nice from 1917 until his death. His earlier works were inspired by the vivid light and colours of the Riviera. During World War II he retreated to Vence, where he designed the unique Chapelle du Rosaire *(p47)*, and its Stations of the Cross, vestments and furnishings.

6 Raoul Dufy

Dufy (1877–1953) embodies the values of the Fauvist school, with its revolutionary use of bright, intense colour. He found Nice the perfect background for his vivid work.

Van Gogh's *The Red Vineyard Near Arles* (1888)

Fernand Léger photographed in his studio in 1955

7 Fernand Léger

Léger (1881–1955) is known for his strong Cubist paintings and his love of bold lines and pure primary colours. He devoted the later years of his life to working in ceramics in Biot *(p117)*, and eventually bought a villa in the village.

8 Pablo Picasso

Picasso (1881–1973) was influenced by the sights and colours of Provence, where he lived in exile from his native Spain for much of his life. He learned to make ceramics from the potters of Vallauris *(p112)* and helped revive the craft.

9 Marc Chagall

The Russian-born painter (1887–1985) moved to St-Paul-de-Vence *(p40)* in 1949. His light-filled work was often inspired by biblical themes. Canvases from his *Biblical Message* series of paintings are in the Musée National Marc Chagall *(p48)* in Nice.

10 Yves Klein

Born in Iceland, Klein (1928–62) became one of the leading lights of the Nice School of New Realists, who aimed to create art from everyday materials. His *Anthropométries*, in Nice's Musée d'Art Moderne et d'Art Contemporain *(p101)*, was created by three nude women, covered in his signature blue paint, rolling over a huge white canvas.

TOP 10 WRITERS IN PROVENCE

1. Alexandre Dumas (1802–70)
Dumas used the Château d'If *(p82)* as the grim backdrop to *The Count of Monte Cristo* (1845).

2. Frédéric Mistral (1830–1914)
This Nobel Prize-winner wrote epic poems based on local lore.

3. Alphonse Daudet (1849–97)
Daudet is best remembered for *Tartarin de Tarascon*.

4. Edith Wharton (1862–1937)
Wharton spent winters at her villa in Hyères, where she finished *The Age of Innocence*, the first book by a woman to win the Pulitzer Prize.

5. Colette (1873–1954)
Colette wrote about St-Tropez in *La Naissance du Jour* (1928).

6. Jean Giono (1895–1970)
Born in Manosque, this son of Provence wrote lyrically about the region's people and landscapes.

7. Marcel Pagnol (1895–1974)
Author and film director, Pagnol wrote *L'Eau des Collines* (1963), later filmed as *Jean de Florette* and *Manon des Sources*.

8. F Scott Fitzgerald (1896–1940)
The US writer stayed at Juan-les-Pins in 1926 while he wrote his novel *Tender is the Night*.

9. Albert Camus (1913–60)
This French author and existentialist wrote his respected autobiography at Lourmarin.

10. Graham Greene (1914–91)
The English novelist retired to Nice, where he wrote *J'Accuse – the Dark Side of Nice* (1982).

French writer Colette

PROVENÇAL LEGENDS

1 Roussillon

The red cliffs of Roussillon *(p133)* are not coloured by accident. In medieval times the local lord's wife, Sirmonde, fell in love with a troubadour. The lord had him killed and Sirmonde threw herself off a cliff, staining the rocks with her blood.

2 Man in the Iron Mask

Who was the Man in the Iron Mask? Louis XIV's troublesome brother? A meddling royal priest? No one knows. Certainly, he was dangerous enough to be clamped in a mask and locked from 1687 on Île Ste-Marguerite *(p76)*. You may visit the island fort *(p82)* and see his cell.

3 Avignon's Hidden Treasure

Pope John XXII was rumoured to be an alchemist, who used magic to win his election. He had an amulet to detect poison (supposedly because other churchmen kept trying to kill him) and made enough gold to fill an underground room. When Benedict XIII, the last Avignon anti-pope *(p23)*, was forced to flee, he walled the room up. The room, with its treasure, has never been found.

4 Pont d'Avignon

In 1177, a shepherd boy named Bénézet received orders from God that a bridge *(p132)* should be built across the Rhône. Avignon people were sceptical, so the lad picked up a rock that 30 strong men couldn't shift and carried it to where Pont St-Bénézet, known as Pont d'Avignon today, was to begin.

5 St Maximin-la-Ste-Baume

After reputedly landing in Provence, Mary Magdalene spread the Christian word, before spending her last years praying in a cave in the Ste-Baume mountains. Her remains were discovered in the 13th century and may be seen in a reliquary in the Gothic basilica *(p95)*.

6 Catherine Ségurane, Nice

Washerwoman Cathérine led Niçois resistance against the Turkish fleet that besieged the city in 1543. She knocked out the Turkish standard-bearer with her washboard, before lifting her skirts and putting the rest of the Turks to flight. The battle was eventually lost, but Cathérine has a statue in Vieux Nice *(p30)*.

7 Les Pénitents des Mées

In 800 CE, a group of monks ogled female Saracen prisoners being led to the Durance river and were turned to

stone as punishment *(p126)*. There they remain – a 2-km (1-mile) line of rocks, some 100 m (300 ft) high, looking like repentant monks with their cowls up.

8 Saintes-Maries-de-la-Mer

After being set adrift in a boat from Palestine, Mary Jacoby (sister of the Virgin Mary), Mary Magdalene, Mary Salome, Lazarus and a servant girl, Sara, landed on the Provençal coast. They were the first Christians in Gaul. The "relics" of Jacoby and Salome are found in the church *(p90)*, as are those of Sara, patron saint of the Romani people.

9 Lost "City of God"

The Latin inscription on a rock near St-Geniez indicates the site of a 5th-century "Theopolis", or City of God. No other trace has ever been found. However, phenomena here, including strange lights and odd weather, add to the mystery.

10 La Tarasque, Tarascon

The Tarasque, a dragon-like beast, terrorized Tarascon in the 1st century CE, until St Martha sprinkled it with holy water. The Tarasque remains central to the town's lively June festival.

Famous Pont d'Avignon, straddling the Rhône

TOP 10 TRADITIONS

A Tarasque being paraded

1. Les Tripettes, Barjols
E4
Les Tripettes takes place in January to mark the end of a 14th-century famine.

2. Corso Fleuri, Bormes-les-Mimosas
E5
Annual flower parade *(p96)* celebrating mimosas and spring blooms.

3. Fête de la Transhumance, Riez
E3
Sheep are led through the town as they move to an upland pasture on the third or fourth Sunday in June.

4. Fête de la St-Jean, Valréas
B2
A boy is elected to "protect" the town on the third or fourth weekend in June.

5. Fête de la Tarasque, Tarascon
B3
The fearsome Tarasque "reappears" during the last weekend in June.

6. Fête de la Lavande, Sault
C2
The heartland of lavender celebrates the year's harvest on 15 August.

7. Fête du Millésime, Bandol
D5
This annual event in early December celebrates Bandol's latest vintage.

8. Midnight Mass, Christmas Eve
Pastoral memories mix with Christian ritual, as live lambs join in the Mass.

9. Thirteen Christmas Desserts
The climax of the Christmas Eve meal includes dried fruit and griddle cakes.

10. Nativity Scenes
Depictions of Christ's birth mix biblical characters with traditional terracotta *santon* figures of Provençal villagers.

PROVENCE TOWNS

1 Moustiers-Sainte-Marie

At the entrance to the Gorges du Verdon, Moustiers *(p123)* clings to the soaring rock face like a pendant. The glorious tangle of vaulted streets and tiny squares is divided by rushing streams. High above, tucked against the rocks, is the Notre-Dame-de-Beauvoir chapel. The village is also celebrated for its pottery.

2 Les Baux-de-Provence

Emerging dramatically from its crag on the edge of the Alpilles hills, Les Baux *(p89)* was home to one of the finest courts in medieval Provence. Abandoned for centuries, the ruined castle and labyrinthine streets now throb with summer tourists. But the site remains majestic, the atmosphere lively and the views over mountains and plains quite breathtaking.

3 Sisteron

E2

At the northern gateway to Provence, Sisteron's minuscule vaulted streets and unexpected staircases climb the vast sentinel rock overlooking the Durance river. Atop the crag is an all-but-impregnable 13th-century citadel *(p124)*, which affords unbeatable views over the rugged landscape, including the pyramid-like Rocher de la Baume rock formation to the east.

4 Séguret

Encircling its beautiful hillside like a belt, Séguret *(p133)* stares out from the edges of the Dentelles de Montmirail mountains *(p130)* across the nearby wine plain. It's an almost impossibly pretty spot of tiny, pedestrianized streets, medieval edifices and contemporary artists and artisans.

5 St-Paul-de-Vence

St-Paul-de-Vence *(p40)* was a farming community living quietly within its medieval environs and 16th-century walls until the 1920s. Then it was discovered by the Côte d'Azur artistic community (Picasso, Matisse, Léger) and has been fashionable ever since, with good reason. Both artists and tourists find the tiny streets and ramparts utterly charming.

6 Bormes-les-Mimosas

This delightful village *(p96)* tumbles down the hillside in a cascade of narrow streets. It's a charming jumble of steep alleyways, hidden corners and stone houses adorned with flowers – hence its name. Ascend to the ruined medieval castle at the top of the hill and enjoy the splendid views of the Mediterranean coastline and surrounding landscapes.

Beautiful village of Moustiers-Sainte-Marie

7 Roussillon

Roussillon *(p133)* is perched magnificently above an extraordinary landscape. The mining of ochre and subsequent erosion have sculpted the red-and-gold earth into cliffs, canyons and weird formations. Villagers have applied the local red, yellow and brown ochre to their houses, to enchanting effect.

8 Roquebrune-Cap-Martin

In a winning partnership of the sort only found on the Côte d'Azur, beneath Roquebrune *(p108)* are the grandiose belle époque villas of the super-rich on the Cap-Martin peninsula. Up above are the winding streets, vaulted passageways and 10th-century château of the original village.

9 Fontaine-de-Vaucluse

The "*fontaine*" is actually France's most powerful natural spring – it pumps out 2.5 million cubic metres (55 million gallons) of water a day, and is the source of the River Sorgue. It's a spectacular setting for a lovely village *(p130)*, made even more romantic by its association with the Italian poet Pétrarch, who lived here in the 14th century.

Harbour lined with boats, Cassis

10 Cassis

Cassis *(p88)* is overseen by France's highest coastal cliffs, whose scale reinforces the intimacy of the narrow little harbour and old town centre down below. Its scenic fishing port has long been a favourite among painters. While Cassis now draws crowds to its beaches – with the best swimming in the western creeks – the town remains a fishing port and has retained its original charm.

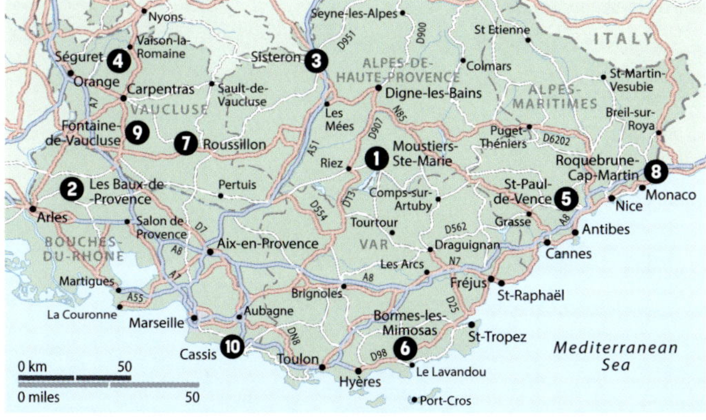

AREAS OF NATURAL BEAUTY

1 Parc Naturel Régional du Luberon

The Luberon region contains a wide range of habitats *(p129)*. The northern mountains are wild and exposed, while the central massif shelters the southern slopes, creating a gentler environment. Moorland, cedar forest, chalk hills and deep river gorges shelter wild boar, eagles, owls and beavers.

2 Gorges du Cians

High in the mountains of Haute-Provence and the Alpes-Maritimes are the ravines of the Gorges du Cians *(p117)* and the Gorges du Daluis, carved by icy, fast-flowing streams descending from wine-red cliffs. At the northern end of the Gorges du Daluis is a large boulder resembling a woman's head, known as the Gardienne des Gorges.

3 Parc National du Mercantour

G2

Spread over 700 sq km (270 sq miles), Mercantour is one of Europe's largest national parks. Its rocky slopes are home to rare species including chamois, ibex, moufflon and marmot. Golden eagles and rare lammergeier vultures can be seen soaring above its peaks.

4 Parc National de Port-Cros

F6 **04 94 12 82 30**

Port-Cros is the smallest of the Îles d'Hyères, and its national park protects it and the 18 sq km (7 sq miles) of sea around it from the development that has overtaken much of the coast. The island shelters beautiful butterflies, rare seabirds and unique plant species, while the surrounding sea offers excellent opportunities for scuba diving *(p62)* and snorkelling *(p97)*.

5 Mont Ventoux

The dramatic peak of Mont Ventoux *(p129)*, at 1,910 m (6,260 ft), seems to guard the gateway to the region. Bare of trees, its higher slopes are known as the *désert de pierre* (stone desert) and are snow-covered from December to April. It has featured in the Tour de France, and even the strongest cyclists dread the treacherous ascent.

Snowcapped mountains, Parc National du Mercantour

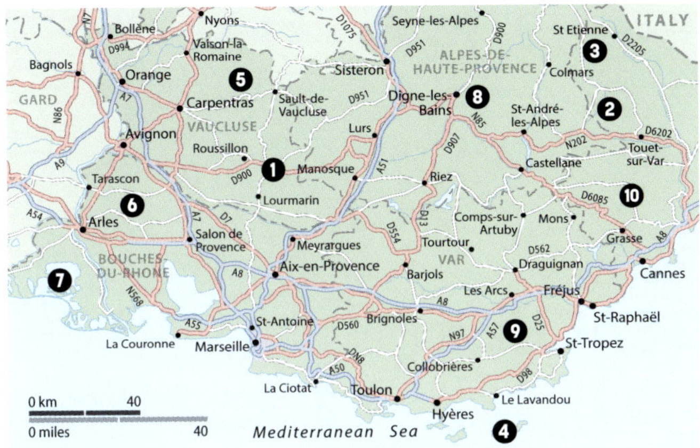

6 Les Alpilles

B4

The chalky hills of the "Little Alps" rise no higher than 500 m (1,640 ft) but display an arid beauty. This miniature sierra stretches for 24 km (15 miles) between the rivers Rhône and Durance, and the GR6 hiking trail which crosses it is one of the finest walks in Provence.

7 The Camargue

This beautiful landscape *(p34)* features lagoons, marshes, wild bulls and France's only cowboys.

8 Réserve Géologique de Haute-Provence

E2

This park in the limestone country around Digne is the ideal spot for dinosaur and fossil enthusiasts. It is the largest of its kind in Europe, covering 1,900 sq km (730 sq miles) of rock, rich in fossils from ancient seas and tropical forests dating back 300 million years.

9 Massif des Maures

E5–F5

Thickly wooded with forests of cork and holm oak, pine, myrtle and sweet chestnut, the dramatic Massif des Maures is wild, hilly and sparsely inhabited, even though it is only a stone's throw from the busy coastal hotspots. It is home to France's only surviving wild tortoises, and makes a welcome change from crowded beaches.

10 Gorges du Loup

The clifftop village of Gourdon *(p120)*, set in rugged limestone country, stands above the dramatic Gorges du Loup *(p118)*, the most accessible of the gorges and canyons that slash through this craggy landscape. The Loup stream plunges over high cascades and has carved deep potholes such as the Saut du Loup ("Wolf's Leap").

Traversing a trail at the Gorges du Loup

BEACHES

1 Plage Notre Dame, Île de Porquerolles

E6

No cars are allowed on the island *(p76)*, so it's a walk or cycleride *(p97)* along the rocky, 3-km (2-mile) track from the port to the loveliest beach in France. Pine-fringed, it has white sand, clear, calm waters, no commerce and few people – your private slice of paradise.

2 Calanque d'En-Vau, Cassis

D5

Calanques (p82) are inlets formed where the chalk cliffs plunge to the sea; many are found between Cassis and Marseille. En-Vau is the prettiest and one of the more accessible – a 90-minute walk from the nearest Cassis car park. At the foot of the white, pine-clad rocks, the setting of sand and luminous sea is intimate, wild and unforgettable.

3 Plage de Pampelonne, St-Tropez

F5

On the largest beach in St-Tropez *(p32)*, famous clubs cater to everyone, from the super-rich to nudists to families. The 5-km (3-mile) sandy stretch across the headland from the town also has extensive public areas. There's space in which to escape the crowds and appreciate natural beauty.

4 Plage de la Garoupe, Cap d'Antibes

Between them, Antibes and Juan-les-Pins have 25 km (16 miles) of coast and 48 beaches, slotted into rocky creeks or opening out into sandy expanses. The prettiest is La Garoupe *(p114)*, on an

inlet of the peninsula. It's highly fashionable and very crowded in summer – but with very good reason.

5 Plage d'Agay, St-Raphaël

As the red rocks of the Esterel hills tumble into the blue sea, they give the coastline around St-Raphaël an untamed allure. The small creeks are enticing; equally appealing, but bigger, sandier and more accessible, is the Bay of Agay *(p110*, which is perfect for families.

6 Plage de l'Eléphant, Le Lavandou

F5

Le Lavandou has 12 beaches covering the full seaside spectrum, from the great sandy stretch of the Grande Plage to the nudist creek of Rossignol. L'Eléphant is the most appealing. The approach is only by sea or over rocks, a feature which usually ensures relative tranquillity.

7 St-Honorat, Îles de Lérins

A short ferry ride leads from the crowds of Cannes to this island *(p77)* owned by Cistercian monks. The presence of the monastery seems to discourage the more brazen holiday-makers so the pretty rock outcrops and tiny beaches here remain calm and, unusually for Provence, positively underpopulated.

8 Calanque de Figuerolles, La Ciotat

D5

Steps on the eastern edge of town lead to this extraordinary creek. On either side are cliffs, while further back are terraces of fig trees and pines. Out front, the blue sea laps around weird rock formations. It is a world unto itself.

9 Plage de St-Aygulf, Fréjus

F5

Long, wide, sandy and safe, the main beach at St-Aygulf, near Fréjus *(p93)*, has the additional advantage of being in a Nature Preservation Area. This protects the Étangs de Villepey – great, wild, freshwater lagoons on the other side of the road, where 217 different bird species have been noted.

10 Piémanson Beach, The Camargue

B5

Thread your way between salt flats and lagoons to arrive at the flat, exposed sands of France's last truly "wild beach". Bordered by small dunes and ponds, this scenic stretch extends for several kilometres across the Camargue landscape.

Relaxing on the sands at Calanque d'En-Vau

GARDENS

1 Jardins d'Albertas, Bouc-Bel-Air

D4 DN8 May, Jun & Sep: 2–6pm weekends and public hols; Jul–Aug: 3–7pm daily jardinsalbertas.com

Laid out in the 1750s, these terraced gardens remain a majestic mix of French and Italian influences – ordered in the geometrical style of France, but with the fountains and statuary favoured by Italy.

2 Jardin de la Villa Ephrussi de Rothschild, St-Jean-Cap-Ferrat

Baroness Rothschild's legendary mansion *(p107)* has extensive gardens, offering exquisite views. These gardens feature eight themed areas, including Spanish, Florentine and Japanese, all richly decorate with plants, sculptures and fountains.

3 Domaine du Rayol, Le Rayol-Canadel

F5 Av Jacques Chirac 9:30am–6:30pm daily (Nov–Mar: to 5:30pm; Jul & Aug: to 7:30pm) domainedu rayol.org

On one of the most magnificent sites on the coast, Domaine du Rayol offers an overview of Mediterranean-style plant life. Gathered around a pergola, a fine mosaic of eight gardens re-creates landscapes of areas of the world with Mediterranean climates. Check the website for information on guided tours.

4 Jardin Botanique des Cordeliers, Digne-les-Bains

E2 Pl des Cordeliers 04 92 30 81 50 Mid-Mar–mid-Nov: 9am–noon & 2–6pm Mon–Fri (Jul & Aug: to 7pm) Wed pm

Named after a 13th-century convent previously on the site, this garden features more than 650 species of aromatic plants from the region and abroad. The plant beds are arranged in classical square design. Note, guided tours are available in English by appointment.

5 Château Val Joanis, Pertuis

D4 D97 10am–1pm & 3–7pm Mon–Sat val-joanis.com

These award-winning gardens were planted in 1978 on three sheltered terraces, mimicking the 17th-century French style. They include a classic potager (vegetable garden) and an orchard amid roses and cypresses.

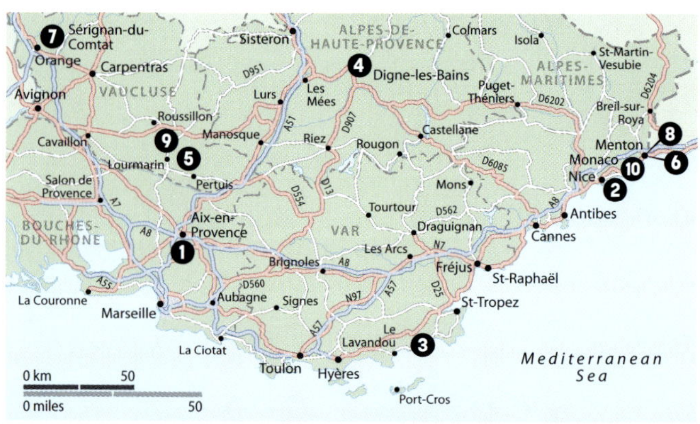

Water garden at the Serre de la Madone

6 Serre de la Madone, Menton

H3 74 rte de Gorbio 10am–6pm Tue–Sun (Jan–Mar: to 5pm) 1 Jan, Nov, Dec menton.fr/Jardin-Serre-de-la-Madone

Anglo-American Lawrence Johnston was a leader among expats who left their mark on Riviera gardens in the early 20th century. His hillside spread is so well landscaped, it barely seems structured. It features terraces that enclose themed spaces or areas dedicated to colourful plants, alongside fountains, water gardens and a collection of statues. Note, guided tours are offered daily at 3pm.

7 Harmas Jean-Henri Fabré, Sérignan-du-Comtat

B2 Rte d'Orange Hours vary, check website harmasjeanhenrifabre.fr

This fascinating walled garden was planted by etymologist Jean-Henri Fabre to observe the lives of insects, which he recorded in exquisite watercolours in his books.

8 Jardin Botanique Val Rahmeh, Menton

More than 700 tropical plants crowd these terraces *(p111)*, established in 1905 by Lord Radcliff, a former governor of Malta. Val Rahmeh specializes in spices, wildflowers, medicinal plants, succulents and rare varieties of tomato and potato.

9 Jardin de la Louve, Bonnieux

C3 Chemin St Gervais 06 03 01 43 12 Hours vary, call ahead Early Oct–mid-Apr

Created by Hermès stylist Nicole de Vésian, this private, ultra-contemporary topiary garden fits in perfectly with the surrounding landscape. Expect a variety of flowers.

10 Jardin Exotique, Monaco

Crisscrossed by winding paths, this garden *(p111)* has a large collection of cacti, succulents and other semi-desert plants – 6,000 varieties in all. A prehistoric cave and anthropology museum are also within the garden grounds.

Cacti in the beautiful Jardin Exotique, Monaco

SPORTING ACTIVITIES

Canoeing on the River Verdon, Gorges du Verdon

1 Canoeing

The classic river trip is to canoe down the Gorges du Verdon – a two-day, turbulent, 24-km (15-mile) trip from Carajuan Bridge to Lac de Ste-Croix *(p24)*. Less adventurous canoeists might prefer paddling the gentler Sorgue, from Fontaine-de-Vaucluse *(p130)*.

2 Sailing

Almost all the coastal resorts have well-equipped pleasure ports and cater for both beginners and experienced sailors. The island of Porquerolles *(p76)* and Bandol village on the mainland have renowned sailing schools.

3 Windsurfing

The breezy Var and Bouches-du-Rhône coasts are ideal for watersports fans. As the Mistral whistles across the Camargue, so windsurfers take advantage at Saintes-Maries-de-la-Mer and Port-St-Louis *(p35)*.

4 Scuba Diving

The richness of marine life, clear waters and a sprinkling of wrecks all draw divers to the Mediterannean coast. The Îles d'Hyères are noted for their seascapes and for the underwater "discovery trail" on Port-Cros *(p56)*. Cavalaire and Marseille remain, however, the best-equipped centres.

5 Golf

The finest golfing *(p97)* can be found at the Frégate golf course, St Cyr, where the sea views are sensational. Other courses offering golf in lovely surroundings include Bluegreen Esterel at St-Raphaël, the Ballesteros-designed Pont Royal at Mallemort and Golf de Châteaublanc outside Avignon *(p130)*.

6 Skiing

Skiing is concentrated where Provence and the Alps meet. In the Ubaye valley, Pra-Loup, Le Sauze and Super-Sauze offer international-standard facilities as, in the Allos valley, do La Foux and Seignus. Meanwhile, there's family-friendly skiing on Mont Ventoux *(p129)* – notably at Mont Serein. In the Alpes-Maritimes, the largest ski resorts are Isola 2000 *(p118)* and Auron, with 45 and 42 various runs, respectively.

Skier on the slopes in the Alpes-Maritimes

Enjoying the thrill of abseiling in a canyon

7 Canyoning

The exhilarating sport of descending torrents and canyons by abseiling, jumping and swimming has taken off big time. Try it in the Roya valley near Saorge *(p120)* or in any of 70 sites in the Ubaye and Verdon valleys *(p24)*. There are some easier descents for beginners in the Pennafort and Destel gorges.

8 Climbing

For some of France's finest, toughest rock climbing, head for the Buoux cliffs in the Luberon *(p129)*, the Gorges du Verdon *(p24)*, with their 933 routes, or the creeks and *calanques (p82)* between Marseille and Cassis. Easier conditions can be found in the Dentelles de Montmirail *(p130)*.

9 Mountain Biking

The marked trails, up and down mountains, through vineyards, forests, gorges and creeks, are endlessly inviting. Figanières is a key centre in the Upper Var, while the Alpes-de-Haute-Provence region has some 1,500 km (900 miles) of marked tracks.

10 Walking

From the coastal paths to mountain tracks inland, Provence could have been created for walkers. Strollers may amble around bays or along woodland paths, while serious hikers can take to the National Hiking Trails (Grandes Randonnées or GR) which crisscross the region.

TOP 10 WALKS

1. Vallée des Merveilles, Parc National du Mercantour
Only serious hikers should attempt this mountain trek. Allow two to three days, overnighting in refuges. Contact Park HQ before setting out *(p118)*.

2. Blanc-Martel Trail, Gorges du Verdon
E3
A 15-km (9-mile) trail in Gorges du Verdon from La Palud to Point Sublime. Allow seven to eight hours.

3. Calanques, Marseille
Explore the *calanques (p82)* by walking along rugged headland trails, which offer breathtaking views and diverse flora.

4. Massif des Maures
The Massif des Maures *(p57)* has excellent trails through its forests, valleys and peaks.

5. Coastal Path, Six-Fours-les-Plages
D6
The seaside walk to La Seyne starts off flat, then climbs to the Cap Sicié for fantastic views. Allow seven hours.

6. Baou de St-Jeannet, St-Jeannet
G4
This stiff but rewarding walk (three to four hours) ascends the *baou* – the rock overlooking the village near Vence.

7. Port-Cros, Îles d'Hyères
Take in a paradise of forests, creeks and headlands as you walk the coast in five hours *(p56)*.

8. Dentelles de Montmirail
The trek from Sablet up to St-Amand, the highest point, takes about six hours *(p130)*.

9. Vieux Nice
From the Old Town up to Colline du Château and down again: the best in-town walking in the region *(p31)*.

10. Massif de l'Esterel
The very best mountain path is from Pont de l'Esterel to Mont Vinaigre. Allow four hours *(p94)*.

FAMILY ACTIVITIES

1 Kayaking, Fontaine-de-Vaucluse

After gushing from its source at Fontaine-de-Vaucluse *(p130)* the river Sorgue becomes idyllic, perfect for a lazy two-hour paddle downstream. Kayak Vert's *(canoevaucluse.com)* canoes hold two adults and two children; life jackets and return shuttle included.

2 Snorkelling, Le Rayol-Canadel

The protected waters off the Var coast offer some of the best snorkelling. In summer, book a guided *sentier sous-marin* (underwater trail) session at the Domaine du Rayol *(p60)* and spot barracudas and even octopuses.

3 Ventoux Aventure, Mormoiron

C2 920 chemin des Salettes
Hours vary, check website
ventouxaventure.fr

Complete with zip lines, suspension bridges, a lake and a small beach, this forest adventure park has plenty to offer tree climbers aged three and above. Beyond the treetops, the view of Mont Ventoux *(p129)* in the background is a bonus.

Whale exhibits in the Musée Oceanographique

4 Azur Park, St-Tropez

F5 Carrefour de la Foux, Gassin
Apr–Sep azurpark.fr/en

Located near St-Tropez, this funfair has 35 attractions, including rides for toddlers. Children will particularly enjoy the prehistoric mini-golf course, featuring model dinosaurs and woolly mammoths.

5 Crossbows and Catapults, Les Baux-de-Provence

Life-sized siege engines – a ballista, catapults, trebuchets and a battering

ram – bring medieval warfare to life at the fortified castle of Les Baux *(p89)*. Special children's activities (including training in shooting crossbows) take place during medieval festivals during the holidays and on summer weekends.

6 Aqualand, Fréjus

F5 Quartier Le Capou, RN 98 Mid-Jun–mid-Sep: 10am–6pm daily (mid-Jul–Aug: to 7pm) aqualand.fr/frejus

One of the biggest water parks in Provence, this offers fun for all ages, from daredevil slides and whitewater thrills to calmer pools and toddler activities in the Children's Paradise.

7 Le Village des Automates, St-Cannat

C4 Chemin de la Dilligence Hours vary, check website villagedesautomates.com

Animated automata bring storybooks to life in a series of themed tableaux, set in a wooded park. Characters include Scheherazade, Gulliver in Lilliput and Pinocchio and the whale. Other attractions here include an adventure park with zip lines, an elevated miniature railway, a tricycle racecourse and a massive indoor playpark.

8 Rocher Mistral, La Barben

C4 Route du Château Hours vary, check website Early Jan–Mar rochermistral.com

The medieval Château de la Barben, the oldest castle in Provence, and its vast grounds are the stage for immersive historical shows such as Rocher Mistral. Actors dressed as peasants, knights, monks and revolutionaries re-enact events from the 11th century to the present day.

9 Les Marais du Vigueirat, Camargue

B4 Chemin de l'Etourneau 9:30am–5pm daily (Apr–Sep: to 5:30pm) Dec–mid-Jan marais-vigueirat.reserves-naturelles.org

Vigueirat has signposted paths and nature tours for ages six and up, with the chance to see white horses, black bulls, pink flamingos, wild boar and more.

10 Musée Oceanographique, Monaco

This museum *(p109)* hasinteractive exhibitions exploring diverse marine life. Its 6-m- (20-ft-) deep aquarium, with over 6,000 species of marine life, is home to sea turtles, sharks and giant rays.

PLACES TO SEE AND BE SEEN

1 La Palme d'Or, Cannes

G4 73 blvd de la Croisette
lapalmedor-restaurant.fr · €€€

The restaurant at the Hôtel Martinez is where stars dine, as the signed photos in the foyer attest, and the menu is suitably opulent. With two Michelin stars, the restaurant offers a fine gastronomic experience.

2 Carlton Beach Club, Cannes

Dipping your toes in the sand, soak in la dolce vita at this chic beach club *(p113)* across the Croisette from the Carlton InterContinental, one of the most luxurious seafront hotels in Cannes. Fancy cocktails and lobster rolls complement the views.

3 Le Petit Majestic, Cannes

G4 6 rue Tony Allard
le-petit-majestic.eatbu.com

This night hangout is popular with the late crowd, who party until the early hours all summer long. During the film festival *(p74)* you'll find all the cream of the world's movie business here.

4 Les Caves du Roy, St-Tropez

To mingle with the rich and famous, book a room at St-Tropez's most stylish hotel, the Byblos, and swan into Les Caves du Roy *(p98)*, the hotel's nightclub. In season, it's the haunt of supermodels, film stars and racing drivers. Wear your most fabulous outfit.

5 Club 55, Ramatuelle, St-Tropez

F5 Plage de Pampelonne, blvd Patch club55.fr · €€€

Ever since Le Cinquante Cinq first opened in 1955, its guest list has read like an A to Z of the rich and famous. Book ahead if you want a table in the restaurant, dress to impress and bring your platinum credit card. Open summer only.

6 Nikki Beach, Ramatuelle, St-Tropez

Join A-listers from Hollywood and Bollywood sipping on cocktails and relaxing on sunloungers to the tunes of top DJs at this glamorous beach club *(p98)*. Open late spring to late summer.

Outdoor seating at the Hôtel du Cap-Eden-Roc

7 Le Bistrot du Port, Golfe Juan

G4 · 53 av des Frères Roustan
Hours vary, check website
bistrotduport.com · €€

The menu at this notable seafood restaurant, presided over by Mathieu Allinei, includes a great bouillabaisse and a variety of fish. The port itself is favoured by Hollywood stars and it is here that Napoleon I made his big, but brief, comeback in 1815.

Entrance to the Hôtel Barrière Le Majestic

8 Hôtel Barrière Le Majestic, Cannes

One of the flashiest café-terraces *(p114)* in town attracts a high-spending, fashionable clientele year-round, and some of the world's brightest stars during the film festival – Robert De Niro, Matthew McConaughey and Jake Gyllenhaal have been sighted. Anything stronger than coffee costs a fortune.

9 Le St-Paul, St-Paul-de-Vence

G4 · 86 rue Grande
lesaintpaul.com · €€

Nestled in a medieval village, Le St-Paul restaurant nurtures the kind of exclusive atmosphere loved by celebrities. Beyond the elegant dining room, the walled garden terrace has tables and comfy wicker chairs surrounding a 17th-century fountain. The cuisine is creative Mediterranean (try the slow-cooked sea bass). At night, the restaurant is pure romance, illuminated by hundreds of flickering candles.

10 Hôtel du Cap-Eden-Roc, Cap d'Antibes

Book years ahead to rub shoulders with high flyers at this luxurious hotel *(p148)*. The model for the hotel in F Scott Fitzgerald's *Tender is the Night* *(p51)*, it was the flagship of Riviera hedonism. The list of celebrity guests stretches back decades and includes such stars as Jennifer Lopez, Gwyneth Paltrow and Leonardo DiCaprio.

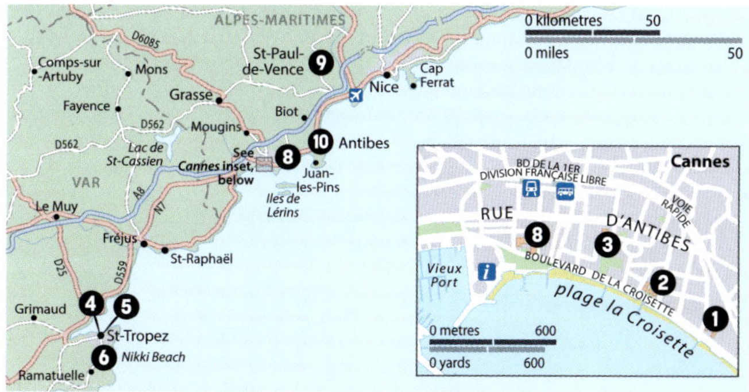

LOCAL DISHES

A stall selling delicious *socca*, a chickpea pancake

1 Socca

A Nice speciality, *socca* is a fried pancake that's made from chickpea flour and olive oil, seasoned with salt and pepper, and pan-cooked in a wood oven. It can be eaten on the go from street-food vendors or pizza-style in restaurants; try it at the excellent La Socca d'Or *(p105)* in Vieux Nice *(p30)*.

2 Bouillabaisse

While this classic seafood stew is now on the pricey side, it started life as the food of the poor. Local fishermen took bony rockfish, which they'd been unable to sell to restaurants or markets, and made t into a stew. Traditionally, the dish must feature at least four of the following: monkfish, red or white scorpion fish, conger eel, spider crab, John Dory, slipper lobster and lobster. Marseille's Les Trois Forts *(p85)* is the perfect place to sample it.

3 Les Calissons d'Aix

Hailing from Aix-en-Provence *(p28)*, these oval-shaped, slightly squidgy biscuits are made from ground almonds and confit melon, and topped with royal icing. They were allegedly invented to celebrate the honeymoon of King René (Provence count) and his bride Jeanne de Laval in 1454. Pick some up from Le Roy Réné, which has several stores in the region, including in Aix-en-Provence.

4 Tapenade

Often found on sale at Provence's markets, tapenade – first invented in the 1880s in Marseille – is made from black olives, capers, anchovies, garlic, lemon juice and olive oil. This spread is often slathered on tartines, crackers and, in Marseille, anything from vegetables to cheese, meat and more.

5 Ratatouille

Made from Provençal summer vegetables – including tomatoes, courgettes and plenty of *herbes de Provence* – this famous French one-pot meal orignated in Nice. Its name comes from the Occitan *ratatolha*, a kind of gruel, and the French verb *touiller*, to stir. Europe's first solar-powered restaurant, Le Présage *(lepresage.fr/wp)* in Marseille, serves a great offering.

6 Aïoli

A mash-up of the Catalan and Provençal words for garlic and oil – two key components in this dip – aïoli is made like a mayonnaise, but the traditional version uses no egg or lemon juice. Sold at markets across the region, including Les Halles d'Avignon *(p72)*, it is an ingredient in several dishes. One of them is *aïoli monstre*, made from boiled vegetables, poached fish, snails and boiled eggs served with generous helpings of aïoli.

7 Tarte Tropézienne

This beloved French sweet treat was created in 1955 in St Tropez *(p32)* at the aptly named La Tarte Tropézienne *(la tartetropezienne.fr/en)*. While the exact recipe for the original has been kept secret, this pastry is always shaped like a giant brioche sandwich, filled with pastry cream and buttercream, and topped with pearl sugar.

8 Pieds et Paquets

Served in many restaurants across Provence, this stew is made from sheep's feet and stuffed parcels of sheep's tripe (stomach) – hence its name, meaning "feet and packages". Added to this are numerous vegetables, herbs and spices, which are then served alongside potatoes. Both Marseille and Sisteron *(p54)* lay claim to the dish, whose origins are said to go back more than 2,500 years.

9 Salade Niçoise

This hearty salad combines tuna and hard-boiled egg with a mix of vegetables, including potatoes, tomatoes, green beans and black olives. Everything is then coated with a dressing made from olive oil, Dijon mustard and white wine vinegar. It may be the staple of *salade Niçoise* now, but when this dish was invented in 19th-century Nice, there was no tuna included. A great place to try it is at L'Escalinada *(escalinada-nice.com/fr)*.

10 La Daube Provençale

The key to this rich, meaty stew is time. First, the meat – typically steak – has to be marinated for half a day with vegetables, garlic, herbs, spices and lemon zest, then it's slow cooked in vinegar, oil and lots of red wine. Head to La Fourchette in Avignon *(p135)* to enjoy a delicious helping.

Servings of rich and hearty *la daube Provençale*

TOP 10 REGIONAL INGREDIENTS

Lavender fields in full bloom

1. Lavender
In bloom from June to early August, lavender is used to infuse everything from soap to honey.

2. Black truffles
Harvested in winter, these "black diamonds" are added to pasta.

3. Wine grapes
There are dozens of Provençal grape varieties, but *ugni blanc* is the most common.

4. Olives
Swathes of the region are dedicated to producing olives and olive oil.

5. Lemons
Grown along the Côte d'Azur, lemons reign in Menton, which has an annual festival celebrating the citrus.

6. Squid
Freshly caught squid is often marinated and cooked in a tomato and garlic stew with capers.

7. Sisteron lamb
Sisteron lamb, from lambs aged 70 to 150 days old, is renowned for its tenderness and slight sweetness.

8. Herbes de Provence
Used in ratatouille, the true mix of these herbs is made from specific percentages of rosemary, thyme, savory and oregano.

9. Camargue salt
The pinkish salt flats *(p34)* produce 500,000 tonnes of salt each year.

10. Banon
This goat's cheese is seasoned with salt, pepper, vinegar and eau de vie, then wrapped in chestnut leaves.

VINEYARDS AND DISTILLERIES

1 Château de Berne

F4 Chemin des Imberts, Lorgues chateauberne.com

British-owned Berne is home to the region's top wine visitors' centre, featuring a full calendar of cultural events, three restaurants and a hotel. The Cuvée Spéciale is its finest wine.

2 Château Ste-Roseline

F4 1854 route de Ste-Roseline, Les-Arcs-sur-Argens sainte-roseline.com

This family-owned estate produces award-winning Côtes de Provence vintages. A medieval abbey adjacent to the château hosts contemporary art exhibitions.

3 Château La Coste

C4 Rte de la Cride, Le Puy-Ste-Réparade chateau-la-coste.com

Irish businessman Patrick McKillen's biodynamic vineyard features a contemporary art promenade with works by Louise Bourgeois and Tracey Emin, among others, and striking buildings by Jean Nouvel, Frank Gehry and Tadao Ando.

4 Domaine Rabiega

F4 Clos d'Ière, 516 chemin du Cros d'Aimar, Draguignan rabiega.com

Set within a wooded residential suburb, this Swedish-run domain has an innovative attitude to wine quality. The Cuvée Clos Dière is among the most expressive of Provençal wines. There is also a chic hotel and a restaurant.

5 Distilleries & Domaines de Provence

D3 9 av St-Promasse, Forcalquier distilleries-provence.com

Home of Henri Bardouin, the connoisseur's pastis. Like all pastis, Bardouin is based on star anise, but here they add 50 other herbs and spices, many of them local. The result is an apéritif more richly flavoured than other brands.

6 Domaine de Beaurenard

B3 10 av Pierre de Luxembourg, Châteauneuf-du-Pape beaurenard.fr

The Coulon family have been here in Provence's most famous wine village since 1695 – time enough to really perfect their skills. The Boisrenard red is the proof. They also run the region's best wine museum.

7 Château de Pibarnon

D5 410 chemin de la Croix des Signaux, La Cadière-d'Azur pibarnon.com

Perched directly above the sea, this may be the most attractively sited

Pretty vineyard at Château de Berne

wine château in Provence. Father and son Henri and Eric have wrestled the unyielding land to produce delicious red wines now in the forefront of the Bandol appellation.

8 Domaine de la Citadelle

C3 Route de Cavaillon, Ménerbes domaine-citadelle.com

Former film producer and politician Yves Rousset-Rouard sank a fortune into this stylish set-up. The Côtes de Luberon wines are treated with respect, and the on-site Corkscrew Museum is unique.

9 Domaine St André de Figuière

E5 BP47, quartier St-Honoré, La Londe-les-Maures figuiere-provence.com

In a superb location, set back from the sea and next to a bird sanctuary, Alain Combard and his family make wines of great finesse. Note that the visitors' entrance to the cellar is round the back of a steel tank.

10 Château Romanin

B3 Mas Romanin, St-Rémy-de-Provence chateauromanin.com

This stunning underground winery resembles a cathedral, and the site has had spiritual associations since the Greeks worshipped here in the 4th century BCE. The owners' methods reflect this past, including cultivation by the phases of the moon.

Bottles of wine in the cellar at Château Romanin

TOP 10 REGIONAL WINES

Beaumes de Venise wines

1. Beaumes de Venise
France's richest fortified dessert wine, made from the Muscat grape.

2. Châteauneuf-du-Pape
At their best, the reds are dark and powerful, while the (rarer) whites are intensely fruity.

3. Bandol
The home of the Mourvèdre grape produces fine and vigorous reds.

4. Côtes-de-Provence
Famed for rosés, this region is now also producing classy reds and heady whites.

5. Gigondas
Sometimes known as "son of Châteauneuf-du-Pape" but the full-bodied wines definitely stand out on their own.

6. Côteaux d'Aix-en-Provence
Fast-improving red and rosé wines, which have floral and citrus notes.

7. Cassis
Fresh, dry whites – particularly good served with Provençal fish dishes.

8. Côtes du Ventoux
The reds, especially, can be very rewarding – although rosés are great for summer picnics.

9. Côtes du Luberon
Another hugely improved group of wines, not least due to investment from fashionable outsiders.

10. Côtes du Rhône Villages
In theory, one step up from ordinary Côtes du Rhône – especially if the name of the village (such as Cairanne) is mentioned on the label.

PROVENCE FOR FREE

1 Contemporary Culture

N1 20 av Stephen Liegeard, Nice 2–6pm (Jul & Aug: to 7pm) Wed–Mon (during exhibitions only) villa-arson.org

The Villa Arson is a fine art school and contemporary art gallery housed in a bucolic villa in northern Nice. Visitors can enjoy a changing roster of exhibitions on contemporary French sculpture, Parisian Pop Art and video montages.

2 Pedalling Provence

Many hotels offer free bike loan for their guests. The region's larger cities, such as Marseille, Aix and Avignon, also have inexpensive bike-share schemes.

3 Vineyard Tastings

Vines have carpeted Provence and the Côte d'Azur since Roman times. Almost every vineyard offers free tastings to visitors amid bucolic grounds – although buying at least a bottle (at bargain château prices) is considered polite. Even the region's finest vintners *(p70)* welcome visitors.

4 Lavender Fields

Blooming lavender fields are best seen from June to early August. Some of the prettiest sights can be seen while driving through Castellet *(p96)*, Gordes *(p133)*, Forcalquier *(p124)* and Sault. The hillside town of Sault draws crowds for the Fête de la Lavande, which is held on 15 August *(p53)*.

5 Church Art

For centuries the Catholic Church was the most powerful economic force in Provence, and it shows in the masterpieces on its walls: visit, for example, Grasse's Notre-Dame-du-Puy *(p46)*, where a Fragonard and a trio of Rubens canvases adorn the interior. But you can see works of interest by the Old Masters for free in almost every church and cathedral in the region.

6 Food Samples

B3 Pl Pie, Avignon avignon-leshalles.com/la-petite-cuisine-des-halles

Every Saturday morning at 11am, one of Avignon's leading chefs cooks up a storm in the city's Les Halles food market. La Petite Cuisine des Halles' programme promises complimentary tastings, recipes and all sorts of culinary tips and techniques.

7 In the Footsteps of Cézanne

Aix-en-Provence's *(p28)* most famous inhabitant is cemented into history with a walking trail. Follow the brass

Stunning lavender fields in Sault, Vaucluse

floor plaques (with an accompanying leaflet if you wish) that lead you through Cézanne's *(p50)* favourite haunts around town.

8 St-Tropez on a Shoestring

Little comes cheap in Europe's A-list getaway. But while the celebs soak up the sun at exclusive Plage de Pampelonne beach bars such as Club 55 *(p66)*, the rest of the shore is free to mere mortals. And Le Café on place des Lices *(p32)* offers guests free use of *pétanque* balls.

9 A Princely View of Monaco

Peer out from the palatial mound of Monte Carlo *(p107)* on a sunny day to glimpse Corsica twinkling in the distance. Whatever the weather, you can see the daily changing of the palace guard at 11:55am.

10 Hiking in Parc National du Mercantour

There are plenty of places in Provence to go hiking, but the beautiful Parc National du Mercantour *(p56)* is one of the best and least crowded spots. Covering a vast swathe of the Southern Alps, this beautiful park is crisscrossed with numerous hiking trails that lead to picturesque Alpine refuges and glacial lakes.

TOP 10 BUDGET TIPS

1. A hotel *petit déjeuner* (breakfast) can cost you upwards of €10. Hit a café for fresh croissants instead, which pair well with a *café-crème* or *café au lait*.

2. Hitchhiking is permitted on all roads except *autoroutes* (motorways).

3. Local wine by the *pichet*, or half-litre carafe, will halve your drinks bill. It's also acceptable to ask for a *carafe d'eau* (jug of tap water).

4. Museum passes are a steal. The French Riviera Pass grants free access and discounts to several sites in Nice and along the Côte d'Azur. Students and over-60s often qualify for a discount, and state-owned museums are free to EU students under 26 (ID is required).

5. Visit sncf-connect.com for train tickets, or thetrainline.com, which also shows Italian train companies operating in France. Rail cards and rail passes are great value.

6. Hotel chains hotelF1 and B&B Hotels offer bargain, no-frills rooms.

7. City-centre self-catering apartments are far cheaper than hotels. The countryside alternatives are *gîtes*.

8. Youth hostels (no age limit) may be found in most major cities and in many national parks. Provençal campsites are not much cheaper than a budget hotel. Wild camping is discouraged.

9. Provençal markets can supply all you need for the perfect seaside picnic at less than the cost of a café terrace snack.

10. Sign up online for one of the region's many city bike-share schemes. Nice's Lime and Marseille's Le Vélo offer bicycles from €1 per hour.

Lime and Pony bikes in Nice

FESTIVALS AND EVENTS

1 Festival de Quatuors à Cordes

Feb

Flower-bedecked floats *(quatours-luberon.org)*, accompanied by live music, are paraded through villages throughout the Var. Among the main processions are those in St-Raphaël and Ste-Maxime.

2 Nice Carnival

Feb

Over 16 days in February, Nice goes wild as multicoloured floats, carnival figures and performing troupes take to the streets. Europe's liveliest event *(nicecarnaval.com)* also features the Battle of the Flowers.

3 Cannes Film Festival

May

Some 30,000 film professionals attend this world-famous gathering *(festival-cannes.com)*, considered one of the most prestigious festivals in the movie industry. As a member of the public, don't expect to meet, or even see, the stars, except as they mount the steps of the Festival Palace for a screening.

4 Fête de la Transhumance, St Rémy-de-Provence

Whitsun weekend

Upwards of 3,000 sheep, as well as goats and donkeys, accompanied by shepherds in traditional costume with sheep dogs, cram into the old village, for a sheep drive (transhumance) to upland pastures.

5 Avignon Festival

Jul

France's greatest theatre event is really two festivals *(festival-avignon.com)*. The official one takes over the Papal Palace's Courtyard of Honour *(p22)* and other venues for both modern and classical drama. However, it is the unofficial "off" festival which enlivens the city, with street performers and up to 400 shows a day, from dance to burlesque comedy.

6 Aix Festival

Jul

Founded in 1948, this is a great lyrical event *(festival-aix.com)*. As well as classical opera in the courtyard of the Archbishop's Palace and other venues, there are more contemporary works, recitals by musicians, music master-classes at its Académie Européenne de Musique and street theatre.

7 Nice Jazz Festival

Jul

Founded in 1948, the best of the region's many jazz festivals draws some of the biggest names in the music business. The festival *(nicejazzfest.fr)* sees 32 concerts over 6 nights on two stages

Spectacular annual parade at the Nice Carnival

in place Masséna, one concentrating on jazz and the other mixing world music, pop and other genres.

8 Chorégies d'Orange

Jul

France's oldest music festival *(choregies.fr)*, dating from 1869, has the town's Roman theatre as its main venue *(p129)*. The original stage wall ensures perfect acoustics for the classical operas that have earned the event an international reputation.

9 International Piano Festival, La Roque d'Anthéron

Mid-Jul–mid-Aug

Since 1980, the festival *(festival-piano.com)* has drawn the cream of the world's classical and jazz pianists to play beneath the plane trees and the night sky at Château de Florans, located in the charming village of La Roque d'Anthéron.

10 Fête de la Véraison, Châteauneuf-du-Pape

1st weekend Aug

Take a step back in time to celebrate the ripening of grapes with villagers dressed in historic costume. Parades, performances and demonstrations of medieval crafts take place over three days of festivities.

Live performance at the International Piano Festival

TOP 10 SPORTING EVENTS

Monaco Grand Prix

1. Paris to Nice "Race to the Sun"
H4 Mar
Watch the final leg of the international cycling year's first major race.

2. Monte Carlo Tennis Masters
H3 Apr
A top tennis event in Monte Carlo.

3. Olympic Sailing Week, Hyères
E6 Apr
Some 50 nations compete in this event.

4. Monaco Grand Prix
H3 May
The one and only street race on the Formula One calendar.

5. Joûtes Provençales, St-Mandrier-sur-Mer
G4 Jun
An unusual sporting event centred on waterborne jousting.

6. Verdon Canyon Challenge
E3 Jun
Tough races through dramatic scenery.

7. Pétanque World Championships, Marseille
K4 Jul
Four days of boules, culminating in a final on the Vieux Port.

8. Feria du Riz, Arles
B4 Sep
Bullfighting, bull running and other festivities welcome the Camargue rice harvest.

9. Les Voiles de St-Tropez
F5 Sep–Oct
Six-day regatta for both traditional and modern sailing boats.

10. Olympique de Marseille
This French football team *(p82)* plays home games August to May.

OFFSHORE ISLANDS

Beachgoers at Pointe du Pin, Port-Cros

1 Port-Cros, Îles d'Hyères

The smallest and most mountainous of the Îles d'Hyères, this national park *(p56)* is characterized by dense pinewoods and oaks. Paths lead up to clifftops, which offer truly dramatic views. For relaxation, La Palud is the best beach.

2 Le Levant, Îles d'Hyères

F6

Although 90 per cent of this island is a French Navy missile base, the other 10 per cent is a naturist colony. Clothes must be worn at the port and in administrative buildings.

3 Ste-Marguerite, Îles de Lérins

G4

Ste-Marguerite offers woods of pine and eucalyptus and stony coves. In 1687, the Man in the Iron Mask was imprisoned in the fort *(p52)* here.

4 Îles du Frioul

C5

The linked islands of Ratonneau and Pomègues guard Marseille harbour *(p80)*. Beyond Port Frioul, white rocks ruggedly conceal unspoiled little beaches. The diving and snorkelling here is renowned.

5 Île d'If

C5 chateau-if.fr

This prison island is most famous as the place from which Dumas' fictional Count of Monte Cristo escaped *(p51)*. You may even visit the "Count's dungeon".

6 Porquerolles, Îles d'Hyères

E6

The largest of the French Riviera islands is the car-free hideaway of Porquerolles. Hire a bike or explore on foot to appreciate this paradise of vineyards, olive groves, scented forests and glorious beaches.

7 Îles des Embiez

D6 lesilespaulricard.com

The larger of two islands developed for tourism by drinks magnate Paul Ricard, Les Embiez is a delight. Development has been sensitively merged into the landscape, leaving most of the island's creeks, woods and salt marshes untouched.

Picturesque setting of Île de Bendor

8 St-Honorat, Îles de Lérins

G4 04 92 99 54 00

St-Honorat has been run by monks almost continually since the 5th century. It features several 10th-century chapels and an impressive 11th-century monastery *(abbaye delerins.com)*. Visitors can leisurely stroll through the vineyards, cultivated by the dedicated monks, and buy the exquisite wine from the shop to take home.

9 Île Verte

D5

The "Verte" of its name refers to the island's lush greenery, notably the trees topping the steep cliffs. Billed as "one of the last virgin islands of the Mediterranean coast", the islet has tiny creeks and beautiful beaches that invite exploration and relaxation.

10 Île de Bendor

D5

With a tiny harbour and scenic beaches, this charming island has also been developed by Paul Ricard and is smaller than Îles des Embiez. However, the tourist development is as sensitive as on Les Embiez, seamlessly complementing the natural landscape while preserving the island's unique beauty and charm.

TOP 10

ISLAND ACTIVITIES

Cycling on Porquerolles

1. Cycling
On Porquerolles and Les Embiez, cycle the forest paths to creeks and beaches.

2. Snorkelling, Port-Cros
Follow a signposted underwater "nature trail" *(p97)* from La Palud.

3. Fort Ste-Agathe, Porquerolles
Mid-May–mid-Oct
porquerolles.com
Browse exhibits on the region's natural, cultural and historical heritage here.

4. Diving, Île des Embiez
Centre de Plongée 06 87 61 03 20
Join diving courses at Île des Embiez to explore its waters, rich with marine life.

5. Lighthouse Walk, Porquerolles
A 90-minute round trip to one of the finest lighthouses.

6. Fort de l'Estissac, Port-Cros
Jun–Sep: 11am–1pm & 3–5pm
Explore exhibits on local history.

7. Aquascope, Île des Embiez
06 23 36 39 55 Apr–Oct
A glass "bubble" over water allows close encounters of a marine kind.

8. Sailing and Sea Kayaking, Bandol
sn-bandol.com
Enjoy sailing and kayaking at Bandol – classes are available in summer.

9. Vallon de la Solitude Walk, Port-Cros
A two-hour walk through shady forest to the Fort de la Vigie.

10. Museum of Wine and Spirits, Île de Bendor
Mid-Jun–mid-Sep: 1–6pm Thu–Tue lesilespaulricard.com
A display of 8,000 bottles from over 50 countries.

AREA BY AREA

Vaison-la-Romaine, Vaucluse

GALERIE
des consuls
V.Ramires

MARSEILLE

Founded more than 2,500 years ago, Marseille is France's oldest city, with historic neighbourhoods such as Vieux Port and Le Panier. Its rich history is also evident in the 16th-century Chateau d'If and the 19th-century Notre-Dame de la Garde. There's plenty of art here, too, including the collection of Mediterranean art at MuCEM and decorative items in the Musée des Arts Décoratifs. Beyond its historical and cultural attractions, the city also offers pretty beaches and a vibrant nightlife scene, with lots of buzzing restaurants and bars.

1 Vieux Port

K4

In 1943, the Nazis attempted to blow up this port, but Marseille remained indomitable. While commercial sea traffic shifted to newer docks in the 19th century, the old port remains the heart of city life. Bobbing with boats and fringed with restaurants, it's where the Marseillais gather for festivities and to buy fish.

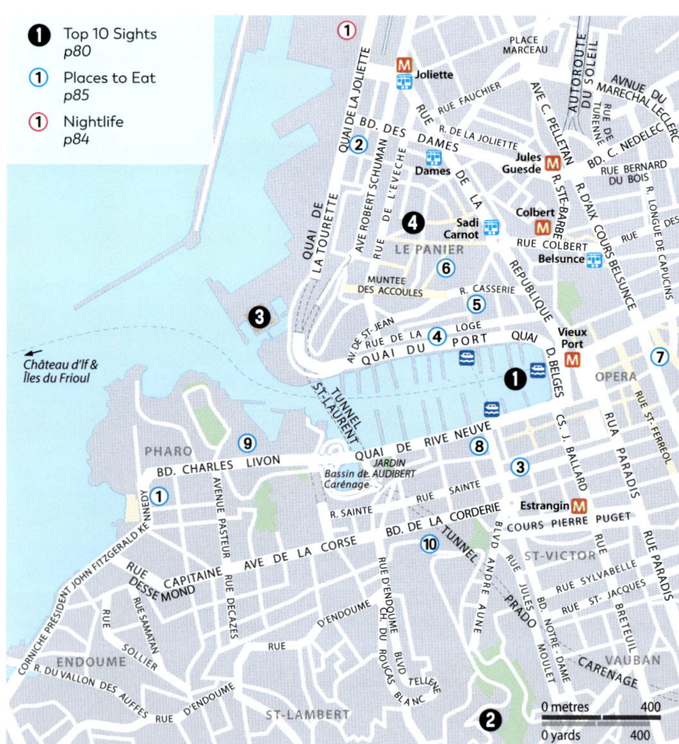

For places to stay in this area, see p146

Notre-Dame de la Garde overlooking the Vieux Port

2 Notre-Dame de la Garde

K6 Rue Fort du Sanctuaire 7am–6pm daily basiliquenotredamedelagarde.com

This Romanesque-Byzantine church is the symbol of Marseille. Perched on the highest hill and topped by a gold statue of the Virgin, it can be seen from everywhere in the city. Built in the 1850s and restored in the early 2000s, its vaulted crypt is carved out of the rock.

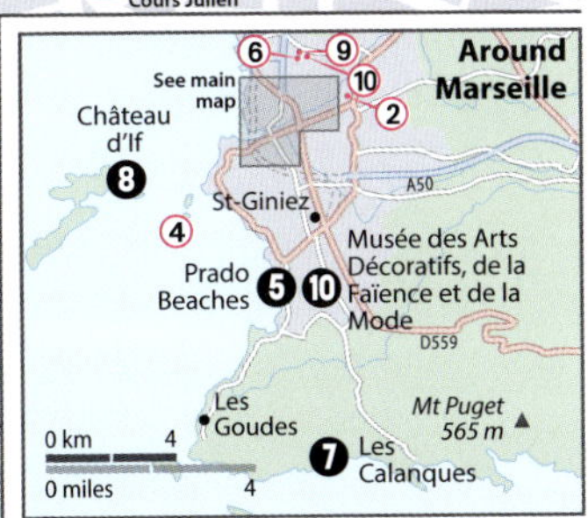

3 Museum of Civilizations of Europe and the Mediterranean (MuCEM)

J4 7 promenade Robert Laffont Hours vary, check website mucem.org

This museum is split between a striking Postmodernist building on the seafront and the adjacent Fort St-Jean. It features art from around the Mediterranean, from Neolithic times to the present day.

4 Le Panier

J3

Marseille's oldest district, Le Panier is located north of the Vieux Port. Originally settled by the Greeks, it later became home to the city's immigrant communities, resulting in a vibrant mix of different cultures. Notable attractions include the 17th-century La Vieille Charité *(musees.marseille.fr)* workhouse, which is now a cultural centre. It is home to the museums of Mediterranean Archaeology and Contemporary Art, and its central chapel features a domed Italian Baroque design. The area is also known for its street art, with walls painted with colourful graffiti, frescoes and murals, creating an open-air gallery. A stroll from Le Panier to cours Julien offers a great opportunity to enjoy this outdoor display.

Kiteboarding on one of the stunning Prado beaches

5 Prado Beaches

C5

Around the corniche from the Vieux Port, past the picturesque fishing port of Vallon des Auffes to the start of the *calanques*, stretch Marseille's modern beaches. They were reclaimed from the sea with earth excavated during the building of the city's metro system. On summer days, they feature every conceivable beach sporting activity; at night, the Escale Borély beach offers some of the city's trendiest nightspots.

6 Palais Longchamp

M2 Blvd Jardin Zoologique 04 91 55 25 51 9am–6pm Tue–Sun Mon & public hols

Longchamp is the greatest expression of Marseille's 19th-century "golden age". What is essentially a water tower is embellished in palatial Second Empire style with fountains, columns and animal sculptures. The central gallery is flanked by two ornate wings, home to the Fine Arts and Natural History museums. Its observatory is considered the oldest scientific building in Marseille.

7 Les Calanques

C5 calanques-parcnational.fr

Within 15 minutes' drive of the city centre you are out of town and into a different world. White rocks plunge into the blue sea and the road winds past *calanques* (inlets) of great beauty. After Les Goudes, access to even more scenic creeks (towards Cassis) is by foot or boat only. To prevent overtourism, visitor numbers to the *calanques* are limited; check the website for details.

8 Château d'If

C5 Hours vary, check website chateau-if.fr

This offshore island *(p76)* fortress, accessible via ferry from Vieux Port,

THE FOOTBALL CAPITAL

Champions of Europe, then embroiled in match-fixing scandals: the history of the Olympique de Marseille football team has matched the turbulence of its home city. But this has not disheartened fans of one of the most popular French teams – football is the lifeblood of Marseille, the Stade Vélodrome its place of worship.

Exploring the courtyard at the Château d'If

was built in the 16th century to protect the city's port and was turned into a prison in 1634. Among its inmates were the real Comte de Mirabeau and Alexandre Dumas' *(p51)* fictional Count of Monte Cristo. Check the website for information on ferry timings.

9 Musée Grobet-Labadié

M3 140 blvd Longchamp For renovation musees.marseille.fr

This museum is in the former private mansion of a rich 19th-century art-loving Marseille family. Its original décor has been retained, re-creating bourgeois life at the peak of the city's prosperity. There's a unique collection of Gobelin and Aubusson tapestries, while the salons have sculptures, paintings, drawings and furniture from the 13th to 19th centuries.

10 Musée des Arts Décoratifs, de la Faïence et de la Mode

C5 134 av Clot Bey 04 91 55 33 60 9am–6pm Tue–Sun 1 Jan, 1 May, 1 & 11 Nov & 25 Dec

Château Borély, a masterpiece of 18th-century architecture, houses an exhibition space for earthenware, ceramics and glass; decorative arts and furniture; and fashion from the 17th century to the present day. It brings together collections from the Musée de la Faïence, Musée Cantini and Musée du Vieux Marseille, along with the furniture from the Château itself. The gardens host outdoor exhibitions and concerts.

Impressive fountain at the Palais Longchamp

A MORNING EXPLORING MARSEILLE

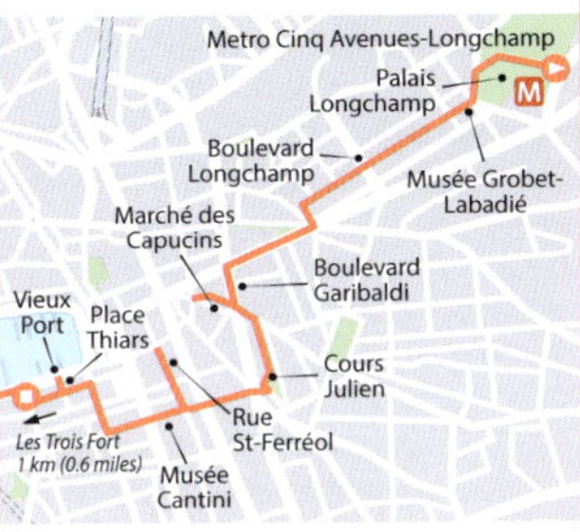

Morning

Start your day at Parc Longchamp *(metro Cinq Avenues-Longchamp)*. Walk through the gardens or explore the museums of the **Palais Longchamp**, found next to the park entrance.

From here, walk towards the centre on the leafy **boulevard Longchamp** (or take the popular T2 tram) to **boulevard Garibaldi**; walk one block south to **Marché des Capucins**, the colourful heart of the city's souk market area; it's also known as the Marché de Noailles *(closed Sun)*.

When you're done with browsing, head east towards **cours Julien**, a lively centre for musicians and artists, full of alternative bars and street art. From the end of the street, take rue d'Aubagne north and then left into rue Estelle. Admire the designer shops in and around **rue St-Ferréol**.

Then visit the **Musée Cantini** *(open 10am–6pm Tue–Sun; closed public hols; adm)* for a magnificent Modernist collection of Fauvist, Cubist and Surrealist paintings.

Rue Paradis brings you to the **Vieux Port** *(p80)*. Stroll to **place Thiars**, a hive of galleries, restaurants and bars, before continuining on to boulevard Charles Livon for a delicious lunch at **Les Trois Forts** *(p85)*.

Nightlife

1. R2 Le Rooftop

J3 Les Terrasses du Port, 9 quai du Lazaret lerooftopdesterrasses.com

Opening early enough to catch the last rays of light, this is Marseille's number one spot for golden hour. Expect tapas, cocktails and crowd-pleasing music.

2. Le Nectar

C5 85 blvd Françoise Duparc

Lovers of organized fun will lenjoy Le Nectar, where every possible activity under the sun takes place. Think comedy shows, live music, blinged-up bingo – you name it, they have it. Check out its socials for the events schedule.

3. Soiffe

L5 8 rue Lafayette 06 89 88 29 22

A half-pint sized microbrasserie and taproom, Soiffe offers some of the friendliest service in the city. The drinks won't break the bank either, especially during their Wednesday and Thursday happy hours (all evening).

4. Île Degaby

C5 Île Degaby iledegaby.com

This 19th-century island-fort, found just off the coast of Marseille, hosts all-day DJ sets from May to October. Entry is by reservation only.

5. Le Pulse

L4 94 cours Julien 04 96 12 08 47

This gay club and bar serves up great vibes and excellent DJs in equal measure. Found in the heart of cours Julien, Marseille's colourful party street, it has a pretty terrace shaded by trees.

6. Le Bar Jo

L1 41 rue Belle de Mai 04 88 10 53 76

A friendly neighbourhood bar in Belle de Mai that hosts frequent concerts. The drinks are great value, as are the home-made, generously portioned dishes.

7. L'art-haché

M4 14 rue de l'Olivier 04 96 12 45 89

Doors open midnight at this late-night party haunt. There's edgy music, retro décor and a great sound system.

8. Prov'oc

M4 8 rue St-Michel 06 17 83 48 44

An excellent wine bar serving gourmet small plates, including grilled mackerel marinated in vermouth.

9. Le Chapiteau

C5 38 traverse Notre Dame du Bon Secours lechapiteau-marseille.fr

An organic bar and zero-waste club with a vast garden and *pétanque* grounds. Activities are mixed with dancing at themed evenings like "dub 'n' *pétanque*".

10. La Friche de la Belle de Mai

M1 41 rue Jobin lafriche.org

This vast events space puts on a smorgasbord of gatherings, including refugee-run foodie events and, in summer, regular DJ sets on the rooftop.

Visitors on the beach at Île Degaby

Places to Eat

PRICE CATEGORIES

For a three-course meal for one with half a bottle of wine (or equivalent meal), taxes and extra charges.

€ under €40 €€ €40–€60 €€€ over €60

1. Restaurant Chez Michel

J5 6 rue des Catalans restaurant-michel-13.fr · €€€

Overlooking Catalan Beach, Chez Michel is known for serving the finest bouillabaisse and other traditional Marseillaise seafood specialities.

2. Le Populo

J3 26 rue Jean François Leca · €

This food court, adorned with street art, offers nine distinct cuisines, ranging from Indian to Sub-Saharan African. It also hosts regular pop-ups and live music.

3. Les Arcenaulx

K5 25 cours Honoré d'Estienne d'Orves Sun les-arcenaulx.com · €€€

Dine in the atmospheric vaults of a 17th-century arsenal at Les Arcenaulx. It is also home to a bookshop and a boutique.

4. Le Souk

J4 98 quai du Port restaurantlesouk-marseille.com · €

Enjoy Moroccan food, especially the tagine and couscous, in a lovely setting with a view of the cathedral.

5. Placette

K4 22 rue de la Guirlande 09 83 53 83 41 · €

Placette is known for its excellent brunch featuring healthy yet delicious dishes and colourful cocktails.

6. 7VB

J4 9 rue Caisserie Sun 7vbcafe.fr · €

This leafy neighbourhood café, with an urban-chic plant-nursery vibe, is widely famous for its mouthwatering sticky cinnamon-and-cream cheese buns.

Fine dining with harbour views at Les Trois Forts

7. La Mercerie

L4 9 cours St-Louis Hours vary, check website lamerceriemarseille.com · €€

This restaurant with a buzzy vibe, run by a passionate trio, serves creative neo-bistro dishes and natural wines.

8. La Table du Fort

K5 8 rue Fort Notre Dame L: Mon, Tue & Sat latabledufort.fr · €€

Close to the Vieux Port, La Table du Fort is run by a welcoming husband-and-wife team. It serves inventive contemporary cuisine made using local produce.

9. Les Trois Forts

J5 Hôtel Sofitel du Vieux-Port, 36 blvd Charles Livon sofitel-marseille-vieuxport.com · €€€

Savour sumptuous seafood dishes at this elegant restaurant while taking in the superb port views.

10. Sépia

K5 2 rue Vauvenargues Mon & Sun restaurant-sepia.fr · €€

Sépia offers a delicious menu focusing on Mediterranean seafood made from the freshest market produce.

BOUCHES-DU-RHÔNE

The Bouches-du-Rhône is full of contrasts. On the coast lies the wetlands of the Camargue, where flamingos and black cattle roam, while north, the streets of Arles are dotted with reminders of Rome's heyday. Aix-en-Provence and St-Rémy-de-Provence have a rich medieval heritage, as do the abbeys of Silvacane and Montmajour and the fortress of Château de Tarascon. You will also find an array of pretty villages, including red-roofed Eyguières and hilltop Les Baux-de-Provence.

1 Roman Arles

Founded by the Romans on the east bank of the Rhône, the city of Arles *(p26)* is the gateway to Provence from the west. Originally established as a naval base, it continues to operate as a river port.

2 The Camargue

Home to a range of rare bird and animal species, this vast expanse of wetlands, salt marshes, lagoons and grazing land is largely protected within the Parc Naturel Régional de Camargue *(p34)*.

For places to stay in this area, see p146

Château de l'Empéri, Salon de Provence

3 Salon de Provence

C4

One of the oldest villages in Provence, Salon is now a busy modern town. Sitting on a hill, it has a historic centre, with medieval buildings, quiet streets and leafy, café-lined squares. The main attraction is the Château de l'Empéri *(p90)* dating from the 9th century. Other places to visit include the museum dedicated to Nostradamus, who lived here in the 16th century, and the Musée de Savon at Savonnerie Fabre, which traces over 600 years of the local olive-oil industry.

4 Château de Tarascon

B3 Blvd du Roi René, Tarascon Hours vary, check website chateau.tarascon.fr

The pale battlements of the Château de Tarascon were built to guard a vital Rhône crossing on Provence's borders; the castle has steep, crenellated curtain walls between massive round towers. It was begun by King Louis of Anjou, ruler of Provence in the 15th century, and was completed by his successor, King René. On his death, Provence became part of France and the castle served as a prison until 1926.

5 Abbaye de Montmajour

B4 Rte de Fontvieille, Arles Hours vary, check website abbaye-montmajour.fr

This massive, fortress-like abbey was built by Benedictine monks in the 10th century. The low hill on which it stands was an island surrounded by marshes and is still known as Mount Ararat. Damaged by fire in 1726, it was restored in the 19th century, and its Église Notre-Dame is one of the largest Romanesque buildings in Provence. Below the church, a 12th-century crypt and chapel have been carved into the hillside.

Ruins of the château at Les Baux-de-Provence

6 Aix-en-Provence

This charming city *(p28)* is a stone's throw from the sprawl of Marseille, but keeps its own identity, with cosmopolitan cafés, a grand cathedral and beautiful 18th-century fountains. Stroll through its leafy boulevards to admire the many 17th- and 18th-century mansions.

7 Cassis

D5

This pretty fishing port, with its brightly coloured boats anchored in a harbour on a rugged, rocky coastline, was a favourite among painters such as Dufy, Derain and Matisse *(p50)*. These artists were inspired by its clear light and Mediterranean hues. Cassis is also renowned for its excellent seafood, with fresh sea urchins considered a local speciality.

Colourful café-lined harbour at Cassis

8 Abbaye de Silvacane

C4 La Roque d'Anthéron
Apr & May: 10am–12:30pm & 2–5pm Tue–Sun; Jun–Sep: 10am–12:30pm & 2–5:45pm daily; Oct–Mar: 10am–12:30pm & 2–4:45pm Tue–Sun
abbaye-silvacane.com

Along with Sénanque *(p38)* and Thoronet *(p94)*, Silvacane is one of the three great sister-abbeys built in the 12th century by the Cistercian order as it rose to prominence in Provence. Its plain, austere architecture reflects the rule of the order, which was founded by St Bernard in protest at the luxury and corruption of other monasteries. The church has a high, vaulted transept and the cloister arcades and refectory were added in the 13th and 14th centuries. Abandoned by its monks in the late 14th century, it became a living abbey once again in the 20th century.

BLACK BULLS AND WHITE HORSES

The wild black bulls of the Camargue *(p34)* are one of the symbols of Bouches-du-Rhône, along with white horses – direct descendants of the prehistoric wild horse of Europe. These are still ridden by *gardians*, the sombrero-wearing cowboys of the Camargue.

9 Les Baux-de-Provence

B4

Perched on a limestone crag, Les Baux is one of the most dramatic fortified villages in Provence. It is crowned by a ruined château *(chateau-baux-provence.com)* with walls that date from the 10th century. Église St-Vincent has 20th-century stained glass by Max Ingrand.

10 St Rémy-de-Provence

B3

Overlooked by the wooded, limestone hills of Les Alpilles *(p57)*, St-Rémy is a perfect exploring base, but it offers excellent sights of its own as well. One of these is the Musée Estrine *(8 rue Lucien Estrine; musee-estrine.fr)*, which has themed exhibitions on Vincent van Gogh *(p50)*, who spent time here, as well as a collection of works by French painter Albert Gleize and temporary exhibitions by modern artists. The town's historic centre also has mansions built in the 15th and 16th centuries. One of them was the original home of the de Sade family, ancestors of the notorious Marquis. It houses the small Musée des Alpilles *(mairie-saintremydeprovence.com)*, displaying artifacts found at Glanum, about 30 minutes' walk from the town centre. Here, the site of one of the most ancient Greek-Roman settlements in Provence is marked by a magnificent triumphal arch and mausoleum.

LITTLE ROME: A DAY IN ARLES

Morning

Visit the largest Roman monument in Provence, **Les Arènes** *(p26)*, for fine views of the historic centre and the Rhône. Next, walk to the **Théâtre Antique** *(p26)* for another glimpse of Roman Arles, then head down to the **place de la République**, which has a fountain with bronze masks, brought from Egypt by the Romans.

On the east, admire the fine Romanesque **Église St-Trophime** *(p47)* and its sculpted pillars crowned by saints and martyrs. Follow the **rue de l'Hôtel de Ville** to **Les Thermes de Constantin** *(p27)*, the remains of a palace built for a 4th-century CE Roman emperor. Then spend an hour in the **Musée Réattu** *(rue du Grand-Prieuré; museereattu.arles.fr)*, with its fine collection of art from the 18th to 20th centuries.

Afternoon

Van Gogh is associated with **place du Forum** *(p27)*, which is cluttered with cafés – one has been painted to look just as it was in his work *Terrasse du Café le Soir*. Stop in for coffee. Finally, visit the **Fondation Vincent van Gogh Arles** *(35 rue du Dr Fanton; fondation-vincentvangogh-arles.org)*, with works by contemporaries highlighting Van Gogh's influence on 20th- and 21st-century artists.

Browsing exhibits at the Maison du Riz

The Best of the Rest

1. Parc Ornithologique du Pont-de-Gau, the Camargue

A4 Pont-de-Gau 9am–6pm daily parcornithologique.com

For a superb view of the Camargue, visit the park, where enclosures display the lagoons' birdlife.

2. Musée de la Camargue

B4 Mas du Pont de Rousty, Arles Hours vary, check website museedelacamargue.com

The Camargue comes to life in this intriguing museum that looks at the delta's history, both natural and human.

3. Maison du Riz, Albaron

A4 Mas de la Vigne Sun–Fri, by appt only maisonduriz.com

Close to the Petit Rhône, this rice museum is run by the third and fourth generations of a family of rice farmers.

4. Pont Flavien

B4

A Roman bridge from Augustus' reign in the 1st century CE, Pont Flavien has beautifully preserved triumphal arches at both ends.

5. Château de Beaucaire

B3 Pl Raimond VII 04 66 59 26 57 Hours vary, call ahead

This ruined 11th-century castle faces the Château de Tarascon. Here, you will find many viewpoints for the Rhône, too.

6. Eyguières

C4

Once the source of Arles' water supply, this village has a 12th-century chapel, a 17th-century church and a ruined castle.

7. Château de l'Empéri, Salon de Provence

C4 Montée du Puech 10am–12:30pm & 2–6pm Tue–Sun Public hols

This 9th-century château was once the seat of the archbishops of Arles. It now houses a museum of military history.

8. Abbaye St-Michel de Frigolet

B3 Montée de Frigolet 8am–6pm daily frigolet.com

This 19th-century abbey has many painted depictions of saints. Guided tours are usually held on Sunday.

9. Abbaye de St-Roman

B3 Chemin de St-Roman Hours vary, check website frigolet.com

This remarkable 5th-century abbey, carved into a rock face, is the only troglodyte monastery in Europe.

10. Église des Saintes-Maries-de-la-Mer

A4 Pl de l'Église 04 90 97 80 25 Hours vary, call ahead

The façade of this 12th-century church features five imposing bells. Inside, it has a 4th-century CE taurobolium altar.

Places to Eat

1. Une Table au Sud, Marseille

C4 2 quai du Port Mon & Sun unetableausud.com · €€€

Run by a husband-and-wife team, this celebrated restaurant is known for its refined and creative cuisine. The restaurant offers an impressive view over Marseille's Vieux Port and the 19th-century basilica.

2. Étude, Aix-en-Provence

C4 24 rue de l'Aumône Vieille Mon & Sun · €€€

A tiny spot with space for just 12 diners, Étude offers an incredibly intimate Michelin-starred experience.

3. La Cuisine des Anges, St-Rémy-de-Provence

B3 4 rue 8 mai 1945 Hours vary, check website angesetfees-stremy.com · €€

The restaurant at this B&B, Le Sommeil des Fées, is a local favourite for lamb tagine and Provençal classics.

4. Le Garage, Martigues

C5 20 av Frédéric Mistral Mon, Sun, Jan (2 weeks) & Aug restaurantlegaragemartigues.com · €

Chef Fabien Morreale serves refined fusion dishes in an Art Deco garage. Note, the menu here changes every month.

5. Le Mazet du Vaccarès, Arles

B4 D37, rte Albaron Villeneuve Mon–Thu mazet-du-vaccares.fr · €€

Located on the edge of the Étang de Vaccarès, this is the place to sample Camargue clams in lemon cream. Note, there are no vegetarian options.

6. Drum Café, Arles

B4 Luma Arles, Parc des Ateliers, 33 av Victor Hugo 04 65 88 10 00 Mon & Tue · €€

This restaurant, located in the Luma cultural centre, is open for lunch only and caters to an artistic crowd.

PRICE CATEGORIES

For a three-course meal for one with half a bottle of wine (or equivalent meal), taxes and extra charges.

€ under €40 €€ €40–€60 €€€ over €60

7. L'Oustau de Baumanière, Les Baux-de-Provence

B4 CD 27 Wed & Thu baumaniere.com · €€€

Superb French cuisine made with local produce sourced from Baumanière's organic vegetable garden.

8. Les Vieilles Canailles, Aix-en-Provence

C4 7 rue Isolette Mon & Sun vieilles-canailles.fr · €€

Locals praise the unpretentious dishes at this laid-back bistro and wine bar.

9. El Campo, Saintes-Maries-de-la-Mer

A4 13 rue Victor Hugo 04 90 97 84 11 Sun D, Mon, Feb–early Mar · €€

Wash down a bull-meat casserole with a glass of Costières de Nîmes, while listening to live gypsy flamenco.

10. Les Maisons Rabanel, Arles

B4 7 rue des Carmes 04 90 91 07 69 Mon & Tue · €€€

The delicious plant-based dishes from chef Jean-Luc Rabanel at this elegant restaurant are a must try.

The exterior of Une Table au Sud in Marseille

THE VAR AND PROVENÇAL COAST

The Var encapsulates all that Provence has to offer. Glitzy St-Tropez, to the south, is the ultimate resort, with smart cafés around its bustling harbour. To the east is the old town of Fréjus, known for its medieval and Roman heritage, while to the west lies the charming Sanary-sur-Mer. Sprinkled across the area are beautiful villages – like forest-encircled Collobrières and fortified Callas – and impressive religious buildings, notably the 12th-century Abbaye du Thoronet. For adventure seekers, the coastal peaks of the Massif de l'Esterel offer numerous trails for exploring.

For places to stay in this area, see p147

1 Sanary-sur-Mer

D5

Lined by palm trees and pastel-hued buildings, the prettiest harbour in the Var remains a busy fishing port, bobbing with boats. There's a morning market held here along the allées d'Estienne-d'Orves, which runs alongside the harbour. Look for plaques nearby commemorating Thomas Mann, Bertolt Brecht and other German writers who took refuge from the Nazis here in the 1930s.

Distinctive Cathédrale St-Léonce, Fréjus Old Town

2 Fréjus Old Town

F5

Fréjus has a striking double heritage. As Forum Julii, it was the second port of the Roman Empire in the region and has some of the oldest remains in Provence. Particularly notable are the elliptical arena and theatre. The town's medieval bishopric status has left it with a remarkable group of episcopal buildings. The 13th-century Cathédrale St-Léonce *(p46)* incorporates a wonderful octagonal baptistry from an earlier 5th-century church and the 14th-century cloisters have ceilings painted with bracingly lurid events from the Apocalypse.

3 Villa Noailles, Hyères

E6 Montée Noailles Jan–Jun & Sep–Dec: 1–6pm Wed–Sun; Jul & Aug: 2–7pm Tue–Wed & Fri–Sun, 3–9pm Thu Public hols villanoailles.com

Built for art patrons Charles and Marie-Laure de Noailles, this villa hosts changing exhibits on design, photography, fashion and architecture.

4 St-Tropez

A longstanding favourite holiday spot for the rich and famous, swanky St-Tropez *(p32)* is known for its buzzing bars and restaurants, as well as its sandy beaches, including Plage de Pampelonne *(p58)*. Despite St-Tropez's popularity, it has retained some of its fishing village charm, seen in the pretty terracotta buildings of the Vieux Port and La Ponche. A highlight here is the Musée de l'Annonciade *(p48)*, which houses a rich collection of early 20th-century French art.

Sprawling 12th-century Abbaye du Thoronet

5 Abbaye du Thoronet, Le Thoronet

E4 Quai Abbaye Hours vary, check website le-thoronet.fr

This 12th-century Cistercian abbey was built in a wooded area near Lorgues. It's one of the finest example of Romanesque architecture in the region, along with its sister houses, Silvacane *(p88)* and Sénanque *(p38)*. The church, the monks' buildings and the cloisters were constructed with unmortared stone and were left bare, creating a simple yet striking space that inspires contemplation.

6 Toulon

E5

Once gritty, this expansive naval port has made a remarkable comeback. Explore the spruced-up old port, take the cable car up Mont Faron for sweeping views and visit the outstanding Musée de la Marine *(musee-marine.fr)*.

Exhibit at the Musée de la Marine, Toulon

PERCHED VILLAGES

The Var's *villages perchés* were built as a defence against Saracen invaders who, in the 9th century, occupied parts of the Var, notably around La Garde-Freinet. Expelled in 973, they returned to wreak havoc at frequent intervals up until the 18th century. The locals therefore took to the hills for protection.

7 Massif de l'Esterel

G4

As the rugged red rocks of the Esterel range plunge into the Mediterranean, they create beautiful creeks. Inland, these volcanic mountains rise no higher than 600 m (2,000 ft) but the landscape is of breathtaking gorges, passes and peaks. Numerous paths and tracks wind through the mountainscape and its rich tree life. Take the Perthus or tougher Mal Infernet valleys – in the footsteps of brigands who hid out here.

8 Caves, Villecroze

E4 Blvd Georges Clemenceau Hours vary, check website grottes-villecroze.fr

Within the rock of Villecroze lie caves that once were home to prehistoric people and, later, provided refuge against Saracen invaders. Most startling, however, is a cave on the

north side of the village, converted by a 16th-century nobleman into a four-storey, fortified house, with Renaissance frontage and carved stone windows. A cascading spring waters gardens below.

9 Basilica St-Maximin, St-Maximin-la-Ste-Baume

D4 Pl de l'Hôtel-de-Ville 7:30am–7:30pm daily During Mass paroissesaintmaximin.fr

Provence's finest example of Gothic architecture was erected for the relics of Mary Magdalene, "discovered" on the site in 1280. From the outside the basilica appears unfinished (there is no belfry), but inside the architecture is striking, with a soaring nave and simply carved columns. Here, there's a 16th-century altarpiece depicting the Passion of Christ and a renowned 17th-century organ. Mary Magdalene's remains are in a reliquary and a marble sarcophagus in the crypt.

10 Musée des Arts et Traditions Populaires, Draguignan

F4 75 pl Georges Brassens 9am–noon & 2–6pm Tue–Sat 1 Jan, 1 May, 25 Dec

Housed in 18th-century buildings in the old town, this is one of the best ethnographic museums in France. Its displays illustrate the story of Provençal life from its earliest days to the beginning of the 20th century.

A DAY'S DRIVE IN THE MASSIF DES MAURES

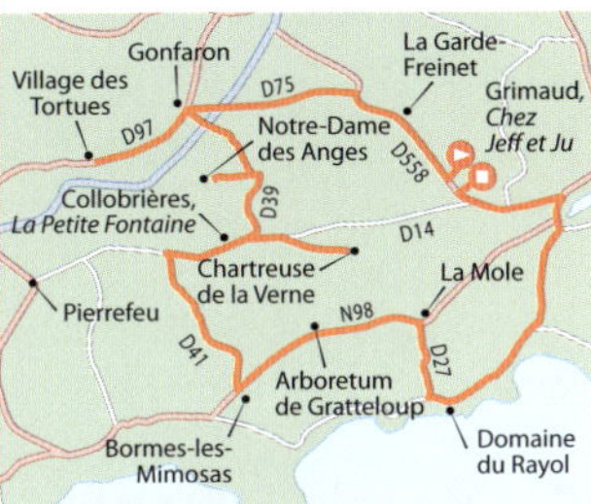

Morning

Start in Grimaud and take the D558 to **La Garde-Freinet** *(p96)*, before driving via the D75 to **Gonfaron**. Turn left onto the D97 to reach the **Village des Tortues** in Carnoules, famous for its rare Hermann tortoise *(open 10am–6pm Wed, Sat & Sun; Nov–mid-Mar: 10am–5pm; adm)*. Head back and take the D39 to Collobrières. At Col des Fourches, head up to **Notre-Dame des Anges**; there's a chapel and fine views.

About 3 km (2 miles) before Collobrières, turn left (D14) to the **Chartreuse de la Verne**, a 12th-century Carthusian monastery *(83610 Collobrières; adm)*. Then double-back to **Collobrières** *(p96)* for a drink or lunch at **La Petite Fontaine** *(p99)*.

Afternoon

Leave towards **Pierrefeu**, but 2 km (1 mile) later turn left (D41) towards **Bormes-les-Mimosas** *(p96)*. This takes you to the N98. Turn left towards La Mole, but stop at the **Arboretum de Gratteloup** (N98), a forest garden.

Continue to **La Mole**, then turn right (D27) to the Col du Canadel and stop at the **Domaine du Rayol** *(p60)* gardens. Returning to Grimaud, enjoy dinner at **Chez Jeff et Ju** *(pl Neuve, Pass du Cros; 07 61 74 29 85)*.

Relaxing at one of the cafés in Tourtour

Var Villages

1. Mons
F4

Almost 820 m (2,700 ft) up, Mons has the heritage to match its grandiose position: ruins of the great Roche Taillée Roman aqueduct run nearby. In the village, narrow alleys wind around ancient porches, pretty arcades and the wonderful 12th-century church.

2. Collobrières
E5

It's difficult to resist a village claiming to be "world capital of candied chestnuts". In the heart of the Massif des Maures *(p57)*, Collobrières is surrounded by forested slopes.

3. Ramatuelle
F5

Despite the overspill from St-Tropez in summer, Ramatuelle remains a lovely hilltop village. Its tiny streets and vaulted passages bloom with flowers.

4. Les Arcs-sur-Argens
F4

With the medieval castle up top, the rest of the old village hugs the rocky promontory. Its labyrinth of streets and vaulted stairways unfold to the modern village below.

5. Le Castellet
D5

This glorious village is accessible only via two gates in its 13th-century walls. Inside, steep, paved streets ascend to a feudal castle, offering outstanding views of olive groves and the sea.

6. La Cadière-d'Azur
D5

The medieval St-Jean gate is a great introduction to this ravishing maze of streets set above the terraced hill-sides and vineyards of Bandol. The panorama here is breathtaking.

7. Tourtour
F4

Remote, perched at 600 m (2,000 ft) up and surrounded by pine forest, Tourtour is a picturesque tangle of streams, medieval buildings and old stone streets leading to a main square lined with restaurants.

8. Bormes-les-Mimosas
E5

A medieval hill village on the edge of the Dom Forest, Bormes-les-Mimosas has flower-lined streets and terracotta-tiled rooftops, plus coastal views.

9. La Garde-Freinet
F5

Nestled amid forests of cork oak and chestnut, La Garde-Freinet stands sentry to the wild Maures Mountains. Higher still are the ruins of the medieval village fortified by Saracens.

10. Callas
F4

Fortified on the side of a green hill, Callas has a winding, self-contained charm imposed by its isolation near the edge of the Canjuers Plateau. It's also a fine base for walking the nearby Pennafort Gorges.

Sporting and Outdoor Activities

1. Watersports

The Var coast offers everything, from sailing and kayaking to windsurfing and parascending. Resorts awarded the "Station Voile" symbol for excellent watersports facilities include Hyères and Bandol. Meanwhile, Brutal Beach at Six-Fours draws international windsurfers and Cavalaire has one of the Mediterranean's best dive sites.

2. Hill Walks in the Maures Mountains

The walking possibilities amid these forests, valleys and peaks *(p57)* are magnificent. The two-hour Collobrières to Chartreuse de la Verne monastery trek is one of the best.

3. Cycling on Porquerolles

Cars are banned on the island of Porquerolles *(p76)*, so cycling is the most rewarding way to explore it. Hire bikes from the village.

4. Mont Faron

E5

Rising 584 m (1,916 ft) behind Toulon, Mont Faron is most easily reached by cable car from boulevard Admiral Vence. The area offers excellent views and walks.

5. Golf

D5 Golf de Frégate, Route de Bandol, St Cyr-sur-Mer

The Var has a dozen golf courses, of which the best known is the Golf de Frégate, set among vineyards and olive groves and overlooking the sea.

6. Snorkelling, Port-Cros

F6

Head to La Palud beach and explore the underwater guided path *(portcrosparc national.fr)* to discover posidonia, coral, mother-of-pearl and brightly coloured fish. It is vital that you contact the Parc National de Port-Cros *(p56)* harbour-master's office before setting out. Remember to use reef-safe sunscreen.

7. Coastal Walks, St-Tropez

F5

Far from the crowds, the paths at St-Tropez wind around creeks and beaches, offering lovely views. The walk from Graniers beach to Cap Camarat takes nearly six hours.

8. Formula One Driving

E5 AGS Formule 1, ZA Circuit du Var, Gonfaron circuitduvar.com

Try your hand at F1 driving with the one-day course, open to all, at the Le Luc circuit – it may be expensive but for petrolheads, it's worth it.

9. Sailing, Lac de Ste-Croix

E3

This vast artificial lake *(p24)* offers all sorts of boating, from pedalo to dinghy. It's also an access point for canoe trips up the gorges.

10. Mountain Biking

Tough-trail cyclists are spoiled for choice in the Var. The most dramatic trips are around the Gorges du Verdon *(p24)* but Draguignan, Figanières and Fréjus also offer challenging, picturesque routes.

Windsurfing competition at a beach in Cavalaire

Var Nightlife

Glamorous outdoor dining area, L'Opéra

1. Les Caves du Roy, St-Tropez

F5 Av du Marechal Foch lescavesduroy.com

The Byblos Hotel's legendary club has a suitably strict door policy: the unfashionable are generally unfortunate. If selected, you will be at the heart of Tropezien nightlife.

2. Nikki Beach, St-Tropez

F5 1093 rte de l'Epi nikkibeach.com

A place to see and be seen, this fabulous beach club has live music and a hedonistic vibe (but it doesn't come cheap).

3. Casino des Palmiers, Hyères

E6 Av Ambroise Thomas hotelcasinohyeres.fr

This casino has retained its belle époque style and added on a glass dome. Alongside the gaming rooms are a hotel, restaurant and nightclub.

4. La Rhumerie, Cavalaire-Sur-Mer

F5 Rue du Port 04 94 05 47 70

With frequent live bands and theme nights, this lively cocktail bar rocks the seaside until late.

5. Le Patio, Hyères

E6 12 rue des Marchands 04 89 29 67 88

Choose from 60 rum-based options at this cocktail bar. Pizza is available to order for eat-in or takeaway.

6. Casino de Bandol, Bandol

D5 Pl Lucien Artaud casino-bandol.partouche.com

Play the fruit machines, the tables – or the field – at this stylish complex, which also has an elegant restaurant and a sleek lounge bar, both with great views.

7. Gaïo Restaurant and Club, St-Tropez

F5 4 rue du 11 Novembre 1918 gaio.club

Known for its creative cocktail menu, this restaurant-club hybrid is expensive, but not excessively so for St-Tropez. Don't miss the great sushi, elevated with wagyu beef and caviar.

8. L'Opéra, St-Tropez

F5 Residence du Port opera-saint-tropez.com

Since 1962, this waterfront cabaret-restaurant has been a pillar of St-Tropez's jet-set nightlife. Guests can savour global cuisine while enjoying evening performances by flame-throwers, dancers and violinists.

9. Les Moulins de Ramatuelle, Ramatuelle

F5 34 chemin des Moulins lesmoulinsderamatuelle.com

Enjoy apéritifs and a game of *pétanque* at this bar-restaurant, followed by a delicious Provençal dinner. Late-night DJ sets at weekends keep the party going.

10. Bar du Port, St-Tropez

F5 7 quai Suffren barduport.com

Overlooking the marina, this high-tech bar opens for breakfast at 7am and closes late. Lunch and dinner are served before DJ-driven house music kicks in.

Places to Eat

1. Les Viviers du Pilon, St-Tropez

F5 2 av Général-de-Gaulle Nov–Mar viviers-dupilon-restaurant.com · €€

Overlooking the Golfe, this sunny restaurant offers some of the freshest seafood on the coast: the seared tuna with homemade pesto is sublime.

2. Hostellerie Bérard, La Cadière-d'Azur

D5 6 rue Gabriel Péri Mon, Tue, mid-Jan–early Feb hotel-berard.com · €€

Set in a former 11th-century monastery atop a hill, this hotel's on-site restaurant serves innovative Provençal cuisine.

3. Café des Jardiniers, Le Rayol-Canadel

F5 Le Domaine du Rayol, av Jacques Chirac 04 98 04 44 00 D, 2 weeks in Jan · €€

Lunch on soup, omelette and salads, made using fresh produce from lovely waterside gardens west of St-Tropez.

4. La Vague d'Or, St-Tropez

F5 Cheval Blanc, Plage de la Bouillabaisse Thu–Tue L, early Oct–early May chevalblanc.com · €€€

Dining at this three Michelin-starred restaurant promises to be a sensory experience. Try the set menus.

5. La Brasserie, St-Raphaël

F5 6 av de Valescure Mon & Sun, Jan labrasserietg83.fr · €

A hidden gem that serves French cuisine on a garden terrace shaded by lemon and magnolia trees.

6. Hostellerie de l'Abbaye de La Celle, La Celle

F5 10 pl du Général-de-Gaulle Jan, winter: Tue & Wed abbaye-celle.com · €€€

Chef Nicolas Pierantoni uses produce from this inn's organic vegetable garden to create Provençal cuisine.

PRICE CATEGORIES

For a three-course meal for one with half a bottle of wine (or equivalent meal), taxes and extra charges.

€ under €40 **€€** €40–€60 **€€€** over €60

7. La Pomme de Pin, Ramatuelle

F5 Rte de Tahiti Mid-Oct–Mar lapommedepin-restaurant.com · €

Mouthwatering Sardinian fare is served in a convivial setting. Try the *culurgiones*, filled with fresh sheep's cheese.

8. La Colombe, Hyères

E6 663 rte de Toulon, La Bayorre Mon & Tue restaurantlacolombe.com · €€

Enjoy generous portions of refined Provençal cooking and seasonal flavours at this restaurant.

9. La Bastide des Magnans, Vidauban

F5 32 av du Général Galliéni Mon D & Wed D bastidedesmagnans.com · €€

La Bastide takes the simplest local ingredients and comes up with a balanced array of wonderful tastes.

10. La Petite Fontaine, Collobrières

E5 Pl de la République 04 94 48 00 12 Hours vary, call ahead · €

This characterful village restaurant is famous for its excellent, no-frills regional cooking.

The pastel-yellow exterior of La Petite Fontaine

NICE

Fronted by blue seas and backed by mountain peaks, Nice has enchanted visitors since the 19th century, when British, German and Russian aristocrats flocked here for the winter months, building beautiful villas on Cimiez Hill. The city's vibrant light attracted plenty of artists, too, among them Matisse and Chagall, both of whom have museums dedicated to them here. There are plenty of other art museums scattered across the city, including the MAMAC and Musée des Beaux-Arts. At the city's heart lies Vieux Nice, a historic area where labyrinthine streets are lined with buzzing markets, restaurants and bars, and where locals speak their own dialect.

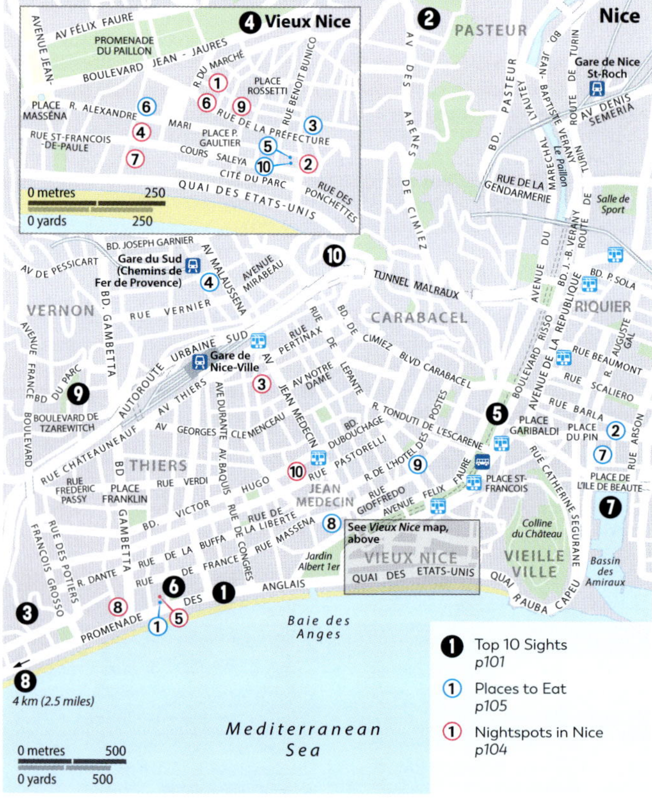

For places to stay in this area, see p147

Playing in the water jets, promenade du Paillon

1 Promenade des Anglais

N5–P5

The promenade des Anglais owes its name to the English community that funded its construction in 1822, in order to give work to the local poor. Now flanked by traffic lanes, it sweeps majestically round the Bay of Angels, dotted with belle époque edifices, notably the magnificent Le Negresco hotel. In contrast, the nearby promenade du Paillon cuts a lush green swathe through the city to the sea and with its central waterway, it provides a tranquil alternative to walking through busy streets. It is also a venue for arts and leisure activities.

2 Musée Matisse

Q1 164 av des Arènes de Cimiez 10am–5pm daily (May–Oct: to 6pm) 1 Jan, Easter, 1 May, 25 Dec musee-matisse-nice.org

Shortly before his death in 1954, Henri Matisse *(p50)* donated a collection of paintings to the city he had lived in for 37 years. They have found a superb home in a 17th-century Italianate villa on Cimiez Hill *(p103)*. Boosted by subsequent donations, the collection affords a comprehensive overview of his work, from 1890 through to the gouache cut-outs of his later years. It is made all the more effective by the display of items from his daily life.

3 Musée des Beaux-Arts

N5 33 av des Baumettes 10am–6pm Tue–Sun (Nov–Apr: from 11am) 1 Jan, Easter, 1 May, 25 Dec musee-beaux-arts-nice.org

The 19th-century townhouse built for a Ukrainian princess is a marvel of Neo-Classical excess. It holds collections of art from the 17th to early 20th centuries. The first floor provides a panorama of 19th-century French art, through to the Impressionists and Post-Impressionists. On the ground floor are 17th- and 18th-century works, including sculptures by Rodin.

4 Vieux Nice

The city's vibrant Old Town, Vieux Nice *(p30)* is famous for its winding streets, Baroque churches and excellent food stalls.

5 Musée d'Art Moderne et d'Art Contemporain (MAMAC)

Q4 Pl Yves Klein For renovation until 2029

Conceived as a triumphal arch on four marble columns linked by transparent walkways, the museum's modern architecture is startlingly effective. The collections trace the story of the avant garde from the 1960s to the present day. Particularly notable are works by the US Pop Artists and European New Realists, including those by Nice's own Yves Klein *(p51)*.

Lush gardens at the famous Musée Masséna

6 Musée Masséna

Q5 65 rue de France 10am–6pm Wed–Mon (Nov–Apr: from 11am) 1 Jan, Easter, 1 May, 25 Dec

This elegant, 19th-century Italianate villa houses the Musée d'Art et d'Histoire, which has a riveting collection covering the period from Bonaparte to the 1930s. Rooms are furnished in First Empire style, and highlights include Napoleon's coronation robe and death mask.

7 Port Lympia

R4

Dug in the 18th century, the port never took off commercially and remains quieter than most city harbours. It is all the more charming for that – a haven of boats and ships, surrounded by Italianate buildings.

8 Parc Phoenix

N5 405 promenade des Anglais 9:30am–6pm daily (Apr–Sep: to 7:30pm)

This themed park, centred around Europe's largest greenhouse, explores world horticulture. Inside this impressive metal and glass "marquee", visitors can wander through re-created warm-climate zones, ranging from an equatorial forest to the Natal desert. The park is also home to the fascinating Asian Arts Museum *(maa.departement06.fr)*. This striking marble-and-glass structure showcases both classical and contemporary creations from the major Asian civilizations.

NICE'S LGBTQ+ SCENE

Nice has a buzzing LGBTQ+ scene, with plenty of gay bars and clubs. The city's calendar is packed with LGBTQ+ events, including Lou Queernaval – France's first gay carnival, whose inaugural event was held in 2015 – in February. Another highlight is the Dolly Party, a street celebration held in mid-August where everyone dresses in white to raise funds for the LGBT Côte d'Azur Centre.

Richly decorated altar at the Cathédrale St-Nicolas

9 Cathédrale St-Nicolas

N4 Av Nicolas II 10am–6pm Mon–Fri, 10am–5pm Sat, noon–6pm Sun During private religious events

In the late 19th and early 20th centuries, the Russian community in Nice was nearly as prominent as the British. This Russian Orthodox cathedral, located in the heart of Nice, highlights the community's influence during that time. Completed in 1912, the chapel within the cathedral was dedicated to the late son of Russian Emperor Alexander II.

10 Cimiez Hill

Q3

When European nobility took to wintering in Nice, they covered Cimiez Hill with magnificent villas in styles ranging from Louis XV to Neo-Gothic. Most impressive of all is Le Régina, where Queen Victoria once stayed. Also on Cimiez Hill is the museum *(p48)* which houses Chagall's 17 great works on the *Biblical Message*. The collection was supplemented by oil paintings, sketches, pastels and gouaches, donated by the artist. Chagall also created stained-glass windows, a mosaic and a tapestry for the museum.

Traditional *pointu* boats lining Port Lympia

A WALK AROUND NICE

Morning

Start at the **Tourist Office** *(5 promenade des Anglais)*, then turn left along avenue de Verdun to **place Masséna**, the city's central square. Take in the glorious red façades, gardens and fountains before crossing to enter **Vieux Nice** *(p30)*. Here, browse the long-established shops on rue St-François-de-Paule, including Auer for confectionery (No 7) and Alziari for olive oil (No 14). Proceed to **cours Saleya** *(p30)* for its famous flower market, then turn onto charming rue St-Gaëtan. Before leaving, visit the **Cathédrale Ste-Réparate** *(p30)*, the **Palais Lascaris** *(p31)*, **place St-François** *(p31)* fish market and the shops on **rue Pairolière** *(p30)*.

Afternoon

In the afternoon head to the 18th-century **place Garibaldi**, then take rue du Dr-Ciaudo to the **MAMAC** *(p101)*. The adjacent Bibliothèque Louis Nucéra was designed as a gigantic human bust with a cube for a head. Continue along **boulevard Carabacel** and admire its stylish mansions.

Shop at **place Magenta**. For designer options, go to rue Paradis then avenue de Suède. Rue de Rivoli brings you to the legendary **Le Negresco** *(p101)*. Treat yourself to dinner its upmarket **Chantecler** restaurant *(p105)*.

The exterior of Bar des Oiseaux at night

Nightspots in Nice

1. Bar des Oiseaux

Q5 Corner of rue St Vincent & rue d'Abbaye Sun & Mon

Francophiles will enjoy the theme nights – philosophy, sing-songs and cabaret – while the rest can sip a drink amid a lively crowd at this colourful bar in the old town.

2. La Civette du Cours

Q5 1 cours Saleya

As the French say, this is *"bar sympa"*, which means a friendly and appealing spot. It's particularly popular with a young, artistic and mildly eccentric crowd.

3. La Cave Romagnan

P4 22 rue d'Angleterre caveromagnan.free.fr

One of the oldest wine bars in town, with live music on Saturday nights and local art on the walls.

4. Le Six

Q5 6 rue Raoul Bosio le-six.fr

In the heart of Vieux Nice, this gay bar has live music, go-go dancers and karaoke every single night in the summer.

5. Le Bar du Negresco

N5 37 promenade des Anglais hotel-negresco-nice.com

The bar of the palatial Le Negresco *(p100)* has a cosmopolitan ambience amid wood panelling and deep armchairs, which give the place the pleasingly laid-back air of a fine club.

6. Wayne's

Q5 15 rue de la Préfecture waynesbar-restaurant.com

Good beer, pub food, live music, table dancing and a terrace – this pub in Vieux Nice is a home-from-home for British expats and tourists.

7. Ma Nolan's

Q5 2 rue St-François-de-Paule ma-nolans.com

The best Irish pub in Nice, Ma Nolan's offers pints of Guinness, home-style cooked dinners, televised sport and free Wi-Fi, making it popular among expats.

8. High Club – Studio 47

N5 45 promenade des Anglais highclub.fr

A popular disco with dancefloors on two levels – the High Club for trendy 20–somethings, and Studio 47 for over-30s in search of a more refined atmosphere.

9. Le Shapko Bar

P4 5 rue Rossetti 07 55 67 89 89

A popular jazz club that features a different band every night at 9:45pm, followed by late-night jam sessions. Arrive early for a good seat.

10. Le Glam

P4 6 rue Eugène Emanuel leglamnice.com

International DJs play techno and house music at this LGBTQ+ dance club, which also hosts drag shows.

Places to Eat

1. Le Chantecler

N5 37 promenade des Anglais Mon, Tue, Wed–Sun L hotel-negresco-nice.com · €€

At Le Chantecler, housed in the iconic Le Negresco *(p100)*, French chef Virginie Basselot serves up Michelin-starred, Provençal-inspired haute cuisine.

2. La Socca d'Or

R4 45 rue Bonaparte restaurant-soccador-nice.fr · €

Enjoy Niçoise specialities like *daube (p69)*, *socca (p68)* and *pan bagnat* (*salade niçoise* sandwich), alongside an extensive pizza menu.

3. Chez Acchiardo

Q5 38 rue Droite 04 93 85 51 16 Sun · €€

Locals sip apéritifs at the counter and from the kitchen comes simple, flavoursome food, like classic *salade Niçoise*. Note, credit cards are not accepted.

4. Racines Bruno Cirino

P3 3 rue Clément Roassal restaurant-racines-nice.com · €€

Vegetables are the highlight of the menu at celebrated chef Bruno Cirino's modern bistro. The weekday set lunch menu offers unbeatable value.

5. Le Safari

Q5 1 cours Saleya restaurantsafari.fr · €€

This family-friendly restaurant offers seafood and meat dishes on one of the liveliest terraces of Vieux Nice.

6. La Merenda

Q5 4 rue Raoul Bosio Sat, Sun, bank hols lamerenda.net · €

Celebrated chef Dominique le Stanc heads up this tiny spot, which serves local favourites like *tripe à la niçoise*. Book ahead and note it's cash only.

PRICE CATEGORIES

For a three-course meal for one with half a bottle of wine (or equivalent meal), taxes and extra charges.

€ under €40 **€€** €40–€60 **€€€** over €60

7. Jan

R4 12 rue Lascaris Mon, Tue–Sat L, Sun janonline.com · €€€

South African chef Jan Hendrik van der Westhuizen wows locals and visitors with his twist on traditional Provençal dishes.

8. Le Boccaccio

Q5 7 rue Masséna boccaccio-nice.com · €€

The décor of this seafood restaurant recalls that of a schooner – but it's stylish, rather than kitsch.

9. Paper Plane

Q4 14 rue Gubernati D, Mon & Sun paperplanenice.com · €

This vegan and vegetarian restaurant offers a brunch-style menu, featuring a variety of pancakes and topped toasts.

10. Le Panier

Q5 5 rue Barillerie Tue & Wed restaurantlepanier.com · €€

Try beautifully presented global dishes followed by delicious desserts such as quince tarte tatin.

Alfresco dining at bustling Le Safari

MONACO AND THE RIVIERA

Stretching from Cannes to the Italian border, the French Riviera has been a luxurious summer getaway for the rich and famous since the 19th century. Here, millionaires dock their superyachts, sunbathers enjoy golden sands, and party-goers dance the night away at Cannes' clubs and bars. The area is known for its beautiful villas, like the Villa Ephrussi de Rothschild, and its art museums, featuring works by artists such as Renoir and Picasso. To the east lies Monaco, an independent state since the 14th century, famous for its lavish Casino de Monte Carlo and the striking Prince's Palace.

For places to stay in this area, see p148

Stately Prince's Palace in Monaco

1 Casino de Monte Carlo

H4 Pl du Casino, Monte Carlo 2pm–4am daily montecarlosbm.com

Built in 1863 by Charles Garnier, this monument to belle époque splendour is also the heart of the region's famous gambling industry – well worth a look.

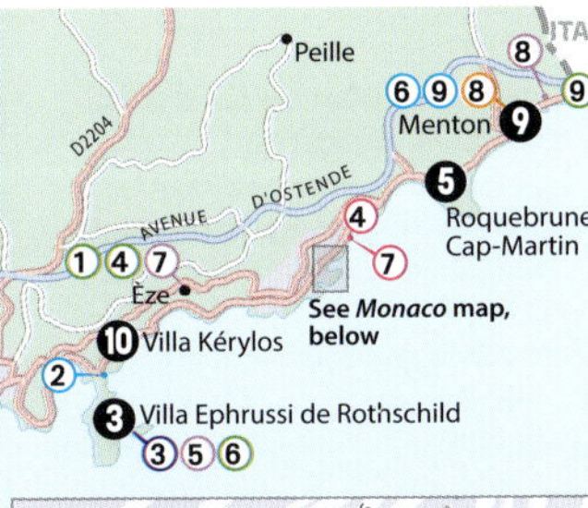

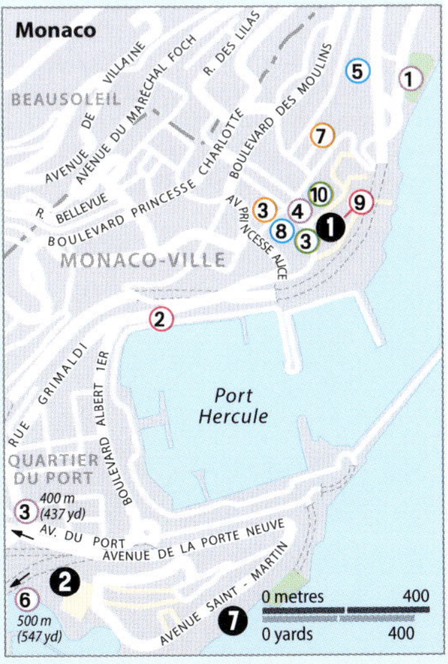

2 Prince's Palace, Monaco

H4 Pl du Palais Mar–Oct: 10am–6pm daily visitepalaisdemonaco.com

Built on the site of a 13th-century Genoese fortress, the Prince's Palace is impressive both inside and out. Highlights include superb frescoes by 16th-century Genoese artists, an opulent Louis XV Salon and a gorgeous Throne Room. Its Cour d'Honneur courtyard features geometrical pebble patterns; here, every day at 11:55am, the changing of the guard is carried out by the Compagnie des Carabiniers du Prince in full dress uniform.

3 Villa Ephrussi de Rothschild, St-Jean-Cap-Ferrat

H4 1 av Ephrussi de Rothschild Hours vary, check website villa-ephrussi.com

The most palatial of Riviera villas, this beautiful building was envisioned by Beatrice Ephrussi de Rothschild, daughter of the famous wealthy banking family. Its Neo-Classical façade conceals an opulent interior of arcades and a covered courtyard adorned with stunning tapestries. The gardens are just as sumptuous as the interior.

Richly decorated state room in the Villa Ephrussi de Rothschild

4 Musée Picasso, Antibes

G4 Château Grimaldi, Vieux Port Mid-Jun–mid-Sep: 10am–6pm Tue–Sun (Jul & Aug: to 8pm Wed & Fri); mid-Sep–mid-Jun: 10am–1pm & 2–6pm Tue–Sun 1 Jan, 1 May, 1 Nov, 25 Dec

A bishop's palace in the Middle Ages, this building then fell into the hands of the Grimaldi lords of Monaco, before becoming the seat of the royal governors of the region. Today, it is an art gallery. The museum houses around 250 works by Spanish artist Pablo Picasso *(p51)*, who worked here in 1946 and donated drawings, paintings and 100 ceramics. Works by other artists, including Miró, Léger, Ernst and Modigliani, are also on display.

5 Roquebrune-Cap-Martin

H3 Pl W Ingram 218 av Aristide Briand; roquebrune-cap-martin.fr

The Château de Roquebrune *(menton-riviera-merveilles.fr)*, perched on its hilltop above Cap-Martin, is said to be the oldest feudal castle in France, built over 1,000 years ago. It has been remodelled often – by the Grimaldi clan and, in the early 20th century, by a wealthy Englishman, Sir William Ingram. At sea level, a lovely coastal path leads all the way to Monaco, passing 19th-century villas in lush gardens.

THE GRIMALDIS OF MONACO

Monaco's Grimaldi dynasty is one of the oldest ruling families in the world. François Grimaldi, disguised as a monk, seized the castle in 1297. By 1489 France and Savoy recognized Monaco's independence. In 1612 Honore II was the first lord to take the title of prince. During the French Revolution the prince and his family were ousted, to be restored to their throne in 1814.

6 Château-Musée Grimaldi, Haut-de-Cagnes

G4 9 pl du Château 10am–noon & 2–6pm Wed–Mon (Jul & Aug: to 1pm; Oct–Mar: to 5pm) 1 Jan, 25 Dec

Built in 1309, this castle's battlements dominate the landscape of Haut-de-Cagnes. Within its walls is a sumptuous palace, built in 1620 by Jean Henri Grimaldi. Today it houses a clutch of museums and art collections, including a museum of modern Mediterranean art, a museum dedicated to the olive tree, and a group of portraits of the 1930s *chanteuse*, Suzy Solidor.

Haut-de-Cagnes as seen from the Château-Musée Grimaldi

Model of a giant squid, Musée Oceanographique

7 Musée Oceanographique, Monaco

H4 Av St-Martin Hours vary, check website musee.oceano.org

Founded by Prince Albert I in 1910, this clifftop museum features rare species of marine plants and animals, including a shark and coral lagoon.

8 Musée Renoir, Cagnes-sur-Mer

G4 19 chemin des Collettes 10am–noon & 2–5pm Wed–Mon (Apr & May: to 6pm; Jun–Sep: to 1pm) 1 Jan, 1 May, 25 Dec

The former home of artist Auguste Renoir has been preserved as it was at the time of his death in 1919. It features 11 of his paintings, along with some of his sculptures and works by his friends Raoul Dufy and Pierre Bonnard.

9 Salle des Mariages, Menton

H3 Hôtel de Ville, 17 rue de la République 8:30am–noon & 2–4:30pm Mon–Fri Public hols

Jean Cocteau decorated this room in Menton's town hall in 1957, adorning it with colourful images of a fishing couple and the story of Orpheus and Eurydice. More of his work can be seen in the two branches of the Musée Jean Cocteau *(p49)*.

10 Villa Kérylos, Beaulieu-sur-Mer

H4 Impasse Gustave Eiffel 10am–5pm daily (May & Oct: to 6pm; Jun–Sep: to 7pm) villakerylos.fr

Theodore Reinach (1860–1928) created this building as a Classical Greek villa, replicating the palace of Delos in Greece. Copies of ancient mosaics and frescoes evoke the Greek city states.

A MORNING TOUR OF THE ROCK

Start this walk around the historical part of Monaco where the Grimaldis founded their principality. Visit the state apartments and the **Prince's Palace** *(p107)*. In one wing is the Musée des Souvenirs Napoléoniens, which houses over 1,000 items, including many of Napoleon Bonaparte's personal effects.

From place du Palais it is a short walk along **rue Basse**, one of the most picturesque streets in the old quarter, to the **Chapelle de la Visitation**, on place de la Visitation. Housed in the Baroque chapel are works by artists Rubens and Zurbaran.

Leaving the chapel, turn right and double-back along **avenue St-Martin** to discover the astonishing sea creatures in the **Musée Oceanographique**. You'll need to allow at least 90 minutes here to view the tanks of marine fauna from all over the world. Don't miss the aquarium with its fearsome sharks. Pause for an early lunch in the museum's restaurant and feast your eyes on the stunning views of the Riviera and the Esterel hills from its terrace before rounding off your visit with the 30-minute ride on the Monaco Tours tourist train. This leaves from the museum on a round trip past the port, the palace, casino and the ornamental gardens.

Palm-lined sandy crescent of the Plage de la Croisette, Cannes

Beaches and Watersports

1. Vieux Port, St-Raphaël

F5

St-Raphaël is the coast's top dive centre, with shipwrecks from World War II and a range of wall dives off the rocky coast. There are several dive outfits at the Vieux Port – a list is available from the tourist office.

2. Plage Helios, Juan-les-Pins

G4 Apr–Sep: 9am–6pm daily

This chic private beach, although it does not offer any watersports, is perfect for lazing on the soft sands.

3. Plage des Fossettes, St-Jean-Cap-Ferrat

H4

Fringed by pine trees, this tranquil beach is popular with locals. Bring a snorkel: there's a variety of sea life to be spotted in the waters here.

4. Plage d'Agay, St-Raphaël

G5

Watersports on this beautiful beach include waterskiing, windsurfing and parascending, as well as more relaxing boat excursions.

5. Plage de la Croisette, Cannes

G4 May–Sep: 8am–sunset daily

One long beach stretches along the Cannes esplanade, sectioned off into tiny private beaches, with parasols, loungers and snack bars. Most of the beaches offer waterskiing.

6. Port Santa Lucia, St-Raphaël

F5

You can try eight different types of watersports here, including parascending, waterskiing and windsurfing, just outside St-Raphaël.

7. Théoule-sur-Mer

G4

The pretty beach at Théoule-sur-Mer, surrounded by hills, bustles in summer. Kayaks, pedalos and more equipment are available to hire.

8. Société des Régates d'Antibes

G4 Quai Nord Port Vauban

8am–sunset daily

This yacht club, with centres in Juan-les-Pins and Antibes, offers windsurfing, dinghy and catamaran sailing and yacht charters for all levels.

9. Plage Belles-Rives, Juan-les-Pins

G4 33 blvd Edouard Baudoin

Jun–Sep: 9am–7pm daily

This hotel beach offers a great range of adrenaline sports that include bungee-jumping and parascending.

10. Plage du Palais des Festivals, Cannes

G4

Perhaps not the most luxurious beach in Cannes, but it is totally free and no more crowded than the paid beaches.

Riviera Gardens

1. Japanese Garden, Monaco
H4 Av Princesse Grace, Monte Carlo 9am–5:45pm (or 6:45pm depending on season) daily
This formal garden is a triumph of Zen horticulture and a striking contrast to most of the classic French gardens of the Riviera.

2. Villa Eilenroc Gardens, Cap d'Antibes
G4 Impasse de Beaumont 10am–4pm Wed & Sat
Charles Garnier, designer of the Monte Carlo Casino *(p107)*, built this villa in a park with trees from all over the world. Note, there are entry charges from April to September.

3. Jardin Exotique, Monaco
H4 62 blvd du Jardin Exotique Feb–Apr & Oct: 9am–6pm; May–Sep: 9am–7pm; Nov–Jan: 9am–dusk 19 Nov, 25 Dec jardin-exotique.mc
The largest collection of succulent rock plants in the world, plus a 60-m- (200-ft-) deep cave with spectacular limestone formations.

4. Casino Gardens, Monaco
H4 Pl du Casino, Monte Carlo 9am–sunset daily
Laid out around the casino *(p107)*, these are classic 19th-century gardens, with trim lawns and water features.

5. Jardin de la Villa Ephrussi de Rothschild
Gorgeous formal gardens and lily ponds surround the pink-and-white villa *(p107)* built by Beatrice Ephrussi de Rothschild.

6. Parc Fontvieille, Monaco
H4 Av des Guelfes Sunrise–sunset daily
Here are palm and olive groves, plus a lake surrounded by 4,000 roses planted in memory of Princess Grace of Monaco.

7. Jardin Exotique, Èze
H4 Rue du Château 8:30am–3:30pm Tue–Sat jardin-exotique.mc
The exotic gardens around the clifftop village of Èze offer superb sea views and an array of unique plant life.

8. Jardin Botanique Val Rahmeh, Menton
H3 Av St-Jacques 9:30am–12:30pm & 2–6pm Wed–Mon (Oct–Mar: to 5pm) 1 May
Laid out by Lord Radcliffe in 1905, this garden is planted with a wide range of subtropical shrubs.

9. Jardin Botanique Thuret, Cap d'Antibes
G4 62 blvd du Cap Summer: 8am–6pm Mon–Fri; winter: 8:30am–5:30pm Mon–Fri Public hols jardin-thuret.hub.inrae.fr
Founded by Gustave Thuret in 1857, this garden showcases an excellent collection of trees and shrubs.

10. Parc de Vaugrenier, Villeneuve-Loubet
G4 Av de Vaugrenier Apr–Oct: 7am–8pm daily; Nov–Mar: 8am–6pm daily
Numerous rare plants can be seen in this park, which also features walking trails and a freshwater lagoon.

Verdant plants at the Jardin Exotique in Èze

Places to Shop

1. Rue d'Antibes, Cannes

G4

For that fabulous Cannes look, head straight for rue d'Antibes and its string of designer boutiques, all breathtakingly expensive and dazzlingly ostentatious.

2. Cours Masséna, Antibes

G4

One of the last original covered markets on the Riviera, cours Masséna bustles with life every morning until noon. It is the perfect place for buying all sorts of local delicacies to take home.

3. Avenue des Beaux-Arts, Monaco

H4

With plenty of cash floating around, Monaco is a magnet for designer shops and haute couture. Try this street, and the allée Serge de Diaghilev, for the latest look.

4. La Croisette, Cannes

G4

Cannes' famous esplanade is an excellent place for shopping or window-shopping, with famous labels such as Chanel (at No 5), Saint Laurent (No 17), Celine (No 43), Louis Vuitton (No 22) and Cartier (No 57).

5. Le Marché Forville, Cannes

G4

This open-air market overflows with flowers, seasonal fruit and vegetables, fresh fish and local products. It's a great place to buy Provençal delicacies to take home. Open daily except Mondays, when it becomes a flea market.

6. Vallauris

G4

Vallauris' moribund pottery industry was revived when Picasso took an interest in the craft. In the summer, more than 100 local potters sell their work on its streets.

7. Metropole Shopping Monte Carlo, Monaco

H4 17 av des Spélugues
metropoleshoppingmontecarle.com

Get the Monaco look at an affordable price at this shopping centre which houses a selection of designer shops selling prêt-à-porter clothes, shoes and accessories.

8. Galeries Lafayette, Menton

H3 Rue de la République

You will find four levels of international designer and brand-name clothes and accessories for men, women and children, all under one roof. There is free parking, too.

9. Antiques Market, Antibes

G4 Pl Audiberti, pl de Martyrs de la Résistance, pl Nationale

Rummage through stalls – selling everything from cut glass and statuary to antique porcelain, lace, embroidery and linen – in search of something small enough to carry home. Thursdays and Saturdays, from 8am to noon.

10. Villeneuve-Loubet

G4

Villeneuve-Loubet supports a thriving arts scene and is full of artists' and sculptors' studios where you can invest in an original work of art by a living artist.

Fresh produce on sale at Le Marché Forville, Cannes

Riviera Nightspots

1. Baoli, Cannes

G4 La Croisette From 8pm Tue–Sat (nightly Apr–Oct and during festivals) baolicannes.com

One of the Riviera's best venues, this cool but expensive club-restaurant attracts the likes of Bono and Naomi Campbell to its Asian-style garden of delights.

2. Equivoque, Monaco

H4 Av d'Ostende equivoquemc.com

A visit to this swanky rooftop cocktail bar overlooking the port is a surefire way to blow your holiday budget. Remember to dress smart.

3. Carlton Beach Club, Cannes

G4 58 blvd de la Croisette carltoncannes.com

Enjoy refreshing cocktails and a Mediterranean menu along with 1950s-style Riviera glamour at this upscale beach club. Relax on the beach, on the central pontoon, at the bar or in the restaurant.

4. Jimmy'z, Monaco

H4 Le Sporting Club, av Princess Grace (00 377) 98 06 70 68 11:30pm–dawn daily

Opened in 1974, Jimmy'z is still one of the most happening places to party in Monaco, attracting the rich, famous and beautiful, and hosting top-name DJs. Of course, all this glamour comes at a steep price. Make sure you dress to impress.

5. Casino Barrière Le Croisette, Cannes

G4 1 Jetée Albert Édouard/1 Espace Lucien Barrière Summer: daily to 5am casinosbarriere.com

Within walking distance of the Palais des Festivals and overlooking the busy Croisette, this casino offers one of the city's largest and most elegant gaming rooms.

Lavish interior of the Casino de Monte Carlo

6. Charly's Bar, Cannes

G4 5 rue du Suquet 06 98 92 40 41

This local favorite continues to draw partygoers with its open-door policy, DJs and dance nights.

7. Blue Gin, Monaco

H4 The Monte Carlo Bay Hotel, 40 av Princess Grace (00 377) 98 06 03 60

As the name suggests, gin is the drink of choice here, with 17 different varieties on offer. Guests can enjoy their drinks on the terrace, which offers sea views.

8. Medusa, Cannes

G4 Pl Franklin Roosevelt medusacannes.com

Set on Cannes' legendary Palm Beach, this glamorous restaurant and club is known for its upscale cabaret performances and cocktails served till late.

9. Casino de Monte Carlo

This casino *(p107)* is the epitome of Riviera glamour, luxury and gambling excess.

10. Chrystie, Cannes

G4 22 rue Macé Sun & Mon chrystie.fr

A restaurant during the day and cocktail bar at night, this is a great place for brunch as well as dancing.

Cafés with Terraces

Outdoor seating at the Café de Paris, Monte Carlo

1. Le Cactus, Èze

H4 7 la Placette lecactus-ezevillage.fr

If your budget won't stretch to the Chèvre d'Or, this modest café has the same stunning views for a fraction of the price and serves delicious crêpes.

2. Hotel Barrière Le Majestic, Cannes

G4 10 blvd de la Croisette hotelsbarriere.com · €€€

Enjoy a glass of wine on this fashionable terrace, which attracts the crème de la crème of the film business during the International Film Festival. It's very pricey – a glass of bubbly here costs as much as a meal in many other spots.

3. Pavyllon, Monte Carlo

This upscale restaurant in the belle époque Hôtel Hermitage has a lush Mediterranean terrace garden overlooking the port, the old town and the sparkling sea.

4. La Chèvre d'Or, Èze

It's worth staying at this gorgeous château hotel just to enjoy breakfast on its clifftop terrace. The ambiance is wonderful, the sea views are breathtaking and the Mediterranean fare is excellent.

5. Le Sud, Cannes

Located in Hotel Martinez, this terrace café offers a chic Provençal village-square ambiance, complete with grapefruit and lemon trees. It is known for its Mediterranean dishes.

6. Villa Ephrussi de Rothschild, St-Jean-Cap-Ferrat

The villa's *(p107)* delightful tea room and terrace, overlooking beautiful gardens and with panoramic views of the bay of Villefranche, is one of the most magical and idyllic places for a light lunch or tea along the entire Riviera, attracting visitors from around the world.

7. Quinto Cielo, Antibes

G4 5 av Saramartel le1932hotelspa.com · €€

This fifth-floor rooftop tapas restaurant at Le 1932 Hotel offers delicious Italian and Spanish cuisine, plus panoramic views over the bay.

8. Plage de la Garoupe, Cap d'Antibes

G4 Sun pm

Walk along the eastern shore of this exclusive part of the Riviera, and you'll come to a short strip of private beaches with several cafés.

9. Mirazur, Menton

H3 30 av Aristide Briand mirazur.fr

The most breathtaking views over Menton and its port are from the lofty garden terrace of the chic restaurant Mirazur, next to the oldest avocado tree in France.

10. Café de Paris, Monte Carlo

H4 Pl du Casino

Set in the Hôtel de Paris, under white umbrellas and blooming flower baskets with the Mediterranean in the background, the inviting Café de Paris is a lovely place for an alfresco meal or a drink.

Places to Eat

1. Maison de Bacon, Cap d'Antibes

G4 664 blvd de Bacon Mon, L Tue & Wed, Nov–Feb maisondebacon.fr • €€€

This legendary fish restaurant has fine views over the beautiful Baie des Anges and serves exquisite seafood dishes.

2. La Table du Royal, St-Jean-Cap-Ferrat

H4 3 av Jean Monnet Hours vary, check website royal-riviera.com • €€€

Housed in the Royal Riviera hotel, this fine-dining restaurant offers elegant, modern cuisine and Riviera views.

3. La Cave, Cannes

G4 9 blvd de la République Mon & Sat L, Sun lacavecannes.com • €€

Since 1989, La Cave has earned a stellar reputation for its excellent bistro dishes and exceptional wine list.

4. Le Vauban, Antibes

G4 7 rue Thuret Mon & Tue, 1 week June levauban.fr • €€

Enjoy perfect renditions of French and Provençal classics in a charming and inviting atmosphere.

5. Pulcinella, Monte Carlo

H4 17 rue du Portier (00 377) 93 30 73 61 • €€

Delicious Italian food is the speciality in this lovely restaurant. Photos of celebrity regulars line the walls.

PRICE CATEGORIES

For a three-course meal for one with half a bottle of wine (or equivalent meal), taxes and extra charges.

€ under €40 **€€** €40–€60 **€€€** over €60

6. Le Rouge-gorge, Menton

H3 5 rue Max Barel 07 49 53 43 43 Sun D • €

At Le Rouge-gorge, enjoy hearty vegetarian and vegan food, often with an Italian influence.

7. La Tonnelle, Île St-Honorat

G4 Île St-Honorat Hours vary, check website tonelle-abbayedelerins.fr • €€€

This restaurant offers splendid views and a fish-based lunch. Wines are made by the resident monks.

8. Le Louis XV, Monte Carlo

The Louis XV. in the Hôtel de Paris, offers a modern culinary experience inspired by the French Riviera.

9. La Petite Cave, Menton

H3 6 pl du Petit Port 04 93 35 90 54 • €

Visit this cosy crêperie for Brittany-style crêpes with a variety of fillings, including Indian and Mexican options.

10. Le Pérousin, Cagnes-sur-Mer

G4 4 rue Hippolyte Guis 09 53 55 61 92 Nov • €€

Known for its seasonal cuisine, this spot offers dishes cooked on an open fire.

Stylish terrace at the Maison de Bacon, Cap d'Antibes

ALPES-MARITIMES

Inland from the Riviera (also part of the Alpes-Maritimes département), the landscape changes dramatically. Here, forested mountains are dotted with charming villages, like the clifftop Saorge, and cut through by deep river gorges, including the Gorges du Cians. The area's rich history can be seen in the Bronze Age art of the Vallée des Merveilles and the Roman monument La Trophée d'Auguste. Notable towns include Grasse, famous for its perfumes, and St-Paul-de-Vence, home to the art-filled Fondation Maeght.

1 Vence

G4

Vence is a gem of the region, with an unbeatable location on a high crag, and sweeping views. The medieval centre is ringed by formidable battlement walls and is entered through a massive stone gateway, to a labyrinth of cobbled streets and tall stone houses. A small cathedral, dating from the 11th century and built on the site of a Roman temple, stands on place Clemenceau.

For places to stay in this area, see p148

La Trophée d'Auguste looming over the town of La Turbie

2 La Trophée d'Auguste

H3 Av Albert 1er, La Turbie
Hours vary, check website
trophee-auguste.fr

This remarkable Roman monument is the only one of its kind still in existence today. Built from limestone, it commemorates the power of Rome and offers fine views along the Riviera. The on-site museum shows a 3D film about the monument's rich history.

3 Biot

G4 biot.fr

Nestled among pinewoods on a hilltop, the pretty little town of Biot is renowned for its high-quality decorative glassware. Visitors can watch the glass-blowing process first-hand at La Verrerie de Biot *(chemin des Combes; verrierebiot.com)*, though an entry fee applies for the museum. Nearby is the fascinating Musée Fernand Léger *(p48)*, which showcases over 400 drawings and paintings by the acclaimed artist.

4 Gorges du Cians

G3

The deep gorge carved through the mountains by the River Cians is made all the more spectacular by the striking red hue of the exposed rock. The river descends 1,600 m (5,250 ft) in just 25 km (15 miles) between the hilltop villages of Beuil and Touet-sur-Var, where the Cians meets the larger river Var. The canyon is at its narrowest and most spectacular at Pra d'Astier, which is about midway between the two villages. Explore the landscape on a rewarding trek or take a scenic drive along the D28 road.

Striking deep-red slate in the Gorges du Cians

Etchings from the Bronze Age, Vallée des Merveilles

5 Vallée des Merveilles

H2

Found high in the Parc National du Mercantour *(p56)*, this valley shelters a treasury of Bronze Age art. Rock carvings dating from 1800–1500 BCE are scattered over the slopes of the 2,870-m (9,400-ft) Mont Bégo. They are difficult to find without a guide, but Musée des Merveilles *(museedes merveilles.departement06.fr)* in Tende displays original and reproduction petroglyphs from the area and puts them in their Bronze Age context.

6 Vallée de la Vésubie

H3 vesubian.com

Two streams merge at St-Martin-Vésubie to form the River Vésubie, which flows through landscapes of pinewoods, meadows, forested peaks and narrow canyons to join the Var 24 km (15 miles) north of Nice. The valley is dotted with pretty villages, and the river is at its most scenic where it passes through the Gorges de la Vésubie, a canyon of coloured rock walls. The area offers a wide range of natural beauty, from lush green forests to glacial lakes and summer snowfields.

7 Forêt de Turini

H3

A moist microclimate, created by warm sea air rising over the cooler mountains, waters this mountain forest, where thick beech, maple and chestnut woods cloak the lower slopes, and huge pines rise on the higher mountainsides. From Pointe des Trois Communes, on the fringe of the forest at an altitude of 2,082 m (6,830 ft), there is a view of the Alpine foothills and the Parc National du Mercantour *(p56)*.

8 Gorges du Loup

G3

In this spectacular canyon, the River Loup has sliced its way deep into the rock to create a series of waterfalls, rapids and deep potholes, including Cascade de Courmes Saut du Loup.

9 St-Paul-de-Vence

This beautiful village *(p40)* inspired some of the greatest artists of the

SKIING IN THE ALPES D'AZUR

High above the balmy coast, the slopes and summits of the Alpes d'Azur are deeply covered in snow in winter, with excellent skiing conditions, and there are more than 250 pistes, ranging from black to green runs, in well-equipped resorts. The best known is Isola 2000, with 3 black runs, 13 red, 22 blue and 7 green.

20th century, including Marc Chagall and Pablo Picasso. Today, its fortified medieval core and charming cobbled streets make it a popular tourist spot. Attractions include the excellent Fondation Maeght *(p48)*, one of the world's finest modern art museums. It displays works by Chagall, Joan Miró and many other 20th-century artists, with its impressive large sculptures in the grounds forming the only permanent displays.

10 Grasse

G4

Once known for its leather-tanning industry, Grasse became a popular perfume centre in the 16th century. The best places explore the history of perfume is the Musée Internationale de la Parfumerie *(museesdegrasse.com)*, which has a beautiful garden of fragrant plants, and the Musée du Parfum *(fragonard.com)*, which features displays of rare perfumery objects like medieval pomanders. Every year in August, the town holds a famous jasmine festival.

Exterior of Grasses' Musée Internationale de la Parfumerie

A WALK THROUGH MEDIEVAL VENCE

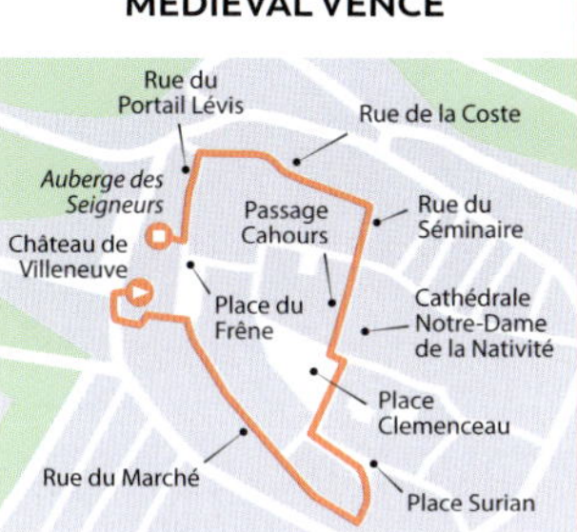

A giant ash tree, Le Frêne (The Ash), marks the beginning of this two-hour stroll through the old quarter of Vence *(p116)*, with its stone-paved streets and medieval houses within a ring of 13th-century battlements. Before entering through the 16th-century Porte du Peyra, visit the **Château de Villeneuve** for modern art and design exhibitions.

After entering the gateway, turn right, and walk along the **rue du Marché** past shops selling herbs, fruit and fresh pasta that will make your mouth water. At the end of the road, turn left and walk across **place Surian** and **place Clemenceau** to the **Cathédrale Notre-Dame de la Nativité** – look out for Roman inscriptions dating back almost 2,000 years on either side of the building, carved when Vence was the Roman settlement of Vintium. Also look for the oak choir stalls decorated with satirical figures, commissioned by a witty 17th-century bishop.

Leave the square by its north side, through the arched **passage Cahours**, then walk up **rue du Séminaire** and turn left to follow the old walls along **rue de la Coste**. Leave the old quarter by the **rue du Portail Lévis**, which takes you back on to **place du Frêne**. There are several dining spots here, like **Auberge des Seigneurs** *(p121)*, where you can enjoy a snack.

Picturesque street lined with stone buildings, Gourdon

Mountain Villages

1. La Bollène-Vésubie

H3

Situated on a forested hillside, this oval-shaped village is encircled by the rugged peaks of Parc National du Mercantour *(p56)*. It's a great place for outdoor activities, including hiking in summer and skiing and snowshoeing in winter.

2. Peillon

H3

Red-tiled houses here seem to grow out of the hilltop itself, rising in tiers to a cobbled square with great views of the forested valley. It has barely changed since the Middle Ages.

3. Puget-Théniers

G3

The village of Puget-Théniers stands where the Roudoule river meets the Var, overlooked by the ruins of the Château-Musée Grimaldi *(p108)*. The 13th-century Knights Templar church *(p47)* here has a beautiful 16th-century altarpiece.

4. Gourdon

G4

From the village square, where the hillside drops into a limestone gorge, you can see all the way down the Loup valley to the coast.

5. Sospel

H3

Colourful arcaded houses and a Baroque church are features of this pretty mountain village near the Italian border. Badly damaged in World War II, the village has been lovingly restored.

6. St-Cézaire-sur-Siagne

F4

Inhabited since the Roman era, this village features medieval walls and watchtowers and is home to the grotto of St-Cézaire *(grotte-saintcezaire.com)*, an underground wonderland.

7. Saorge

H3

This charming clifftop village, full of 15th- to 17th-century houses, offers splendid views and is home to two pretty churches.

8. La Brigue

H2

Unspoiled La Brigue has cobbled streets, arcaded buildings and the Notre-Dame des Fontaines *(p46)*, with superb medieval frescoes.

9. Ste-Agnès

H3

At 671 m (2,200 ft), Ste-Agnès is the highest of the coastal *villages perchés*. There are some great walking trails nearby, in the Gorbio valley.

10. Lucéram

H3

Here, tall old houses are set around a 17th-century Rococo church and an onion-domed clock tower.

Places to Eat

1. Les Terraillers, Biot

G4 11 chemin Neuf Mon, Tue, mid-Oct–Nov lesterraillers.fr · €€€

This sophisticated restaurant is in a 16th-century pottery mill. The dishes are rich and flavourful and the wine list superb.

2. La Bastide St-Antoine, Grasse

G4 48 av Henri Dunant Last week of Feb jacques-chibois.com · €€€

With a Michelin star, this fine-dining spot serves regional dishes on the garden terrace of a charming 17th-century Provençal house.

3. L'Ambroisie, Vence

G4 37 av Alphonse Toreille Mon L, Tue, Wed ambroisie-vence.com · €€

Chef Bruno Seillery serves refined Provençal cuisine in this well-restored former 17th-century chapel.

4. Les Arcades, Biot

G4 14/16 pl des Arcades Mon (winter: also Sun D) hotel-restaurant-les-arcades.com · €€

Run by the same family for three generations, this unpretentious inn is a local favourite. It's decorated with colourful works of art and offers fixed-price menus of traditional dishes such as pistou soup.

5. Hostellerie Jérôme, La Turbie

H3 20 rue du Comté de Cessole 04 92 41 51 51 L, Mon, Sun, Dec–mid-Feb · €€€

Only open in the evenings, this fine restaurant serves inventive dishes such as scampi in a *verveine* crust.

6. Auberge des Seigneurs, Vence

G4 1 pl du Frêne Mon, Sun, mid-Dec–mid-Jan auberge-seigneurs.fr · €

Spit-roasted local lamb and chicken are on the menu at this friendly medieval inn, complete with an open fire.

PRICE CATEGORIES

For a three-course meal for one with half a bottle of wine (or equivalent meal), taxes and extra charges.

€ under €40 **€€** €40–€60 **€€€** over €60

7. La Table de Pierre, Vence

G4 2320 rte des Serres Mon & Sun lemasdepierre.com · €€€

Located in Le Domaine du Mas de Pierre hotel, this opulent restaurant offers fine-dining set menus.

8. Auberge de la Madone, Peillon

H3 3 pl Auguste Arnulf Wed, mid-Nov–Jan aubergedela madone-peillon.com · €€€

Enjoy classic Provençal cuisine on this restaurant's terrace overlooking a medieval village.

9. Les Delicatesses de Grasse, Grasse

G4 3 pl aux Aires 06 16 02 44 26 · €

Small plates, cheese and charcuterie boards paired with different wines make this a popular *apéro* spot with locals.

10. La Farigoule, Vence

G4 15 av Henri Isnard Mon, Tue, late Nov–Christmas lafarigoule-vence.fr · €€

This cosy spot attracts regulars with classic Provençal cuisine.

The medieval inn Auberge des Seigneurs, Vence

ALPES-DE-HAUTE-PROVENCE

In this rugged Alpine region of Provence, the Durance and Verdon rivers have carved deep canyons beneath limestone cliffs, forming an area of exceptional natural beauty. Looming over the landscape are high peaks – among them Mont Pelat and the Montagne de Lure – and mighty fortresses, like the lofty Citadelle de Sisteron and the hulking Fort de Savoie. Elsewhere, scattered here and there across the area, are a number of charming towns and pretty villages, including fortified Lurs and picturesque Moustiers-Sainte-Marie. A highlight of the region is the mighty Gorges du Verdon, a hulking gorge that's a hot-spot for outdoor activities such as hiking, mountain biking and watersports.

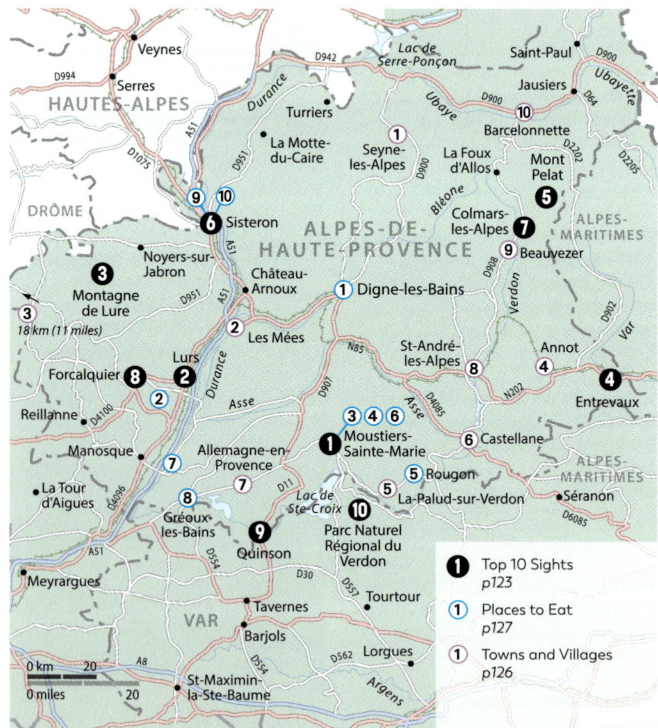

For places to stay in this area, see p149

Stained glass at Moustiers

1 Moustiers-Sainte-Marie

E3

Moustiers, loud with the sound of a swift-running stream which flows through the middle of the village, features tall old houses, plane trees and, for those who can face the climb, a superb view of the Gorges du Verdon *(p24)* from the clifftop church of Notre-Dame-de-Beauvoir. The village is famed for its faïence ware, and you can see examples in the Musée de la Faïence *(musee-moustiers.fr)*; note that there is an entry fee.

2 Lurs

D3

Founded before Charlemagne's reign, during the Middle Ages, the town of Lurs was fortified as early as the 9th century CE, when it was ruled by the bishops of Sisteron and the princes of Lurs. Deserted in the 19th century, it has now become an artists' colony. There are stupendous views from the promenade des Evêques (Bishops' Walk) leading to the chapel of Notre-Dame-de-Vie, especially colourful in spring when the wildflowers bloom.

3 Montagne de Lure

D2

Deep in the heart of the Luberon, the Lure mountain – an extension of the savage massif of Mont Ventoux in neighbouring Vaucluse *(p129)* – is Provence at its wildest, least hospitable and, some would say, its loveliest. Abandoned hamlets are reminders of Provence in the first half of the 20th century, when many rural people gave up trying to scrape a living from this harsh countryside.

4 Ville Forte, Entrevaux

F3

The citadel of Entrevaux is one of the most dramatic of all the region's many fortresses. Perched on a pinnacle above this fairy-tale town, it can be reached only by a steep, zigzag path which passes through more than a dozen arched gateways. Lying beneath it, the impregnable Ville Forte is ringed by towers and ramparts and reached by a drawbridge over the river Var.

5 Mont Pelat

F2

The highest peak in the Provençal Alps rises to a height of 3,050 m (10,020 ft) and dominates a lofty landscape of bare rocky summits, marked by snow until early summer, pine forests and Alpine meadows. The massif is crossed by breathtaking passes, including the Cime de la Bonette, by which the D64 road traverses the shoulder of Mont Pelat at a dizzy height of 2,860 m (9,400 ft), making it the highest pass in Europe.

Hiking through Alpine meadows near Mont Pelat

6 Citadelle de Sisteron

E2 1 allée de Verdun Hours vary, check website citadellede sisteron.fr

Squatting on a steep-sided crag, high above the narrow valley of the Durance river, the formidable defences of the Citadelle guard one of the strategic gateways to Provence *(p54)*. Built in the 13th century, the bastions and ramparts, crowned by towers and a chapel, are a great piece of military engineering. In the summer, they become the venue for the Nuits de la Citadelle, a festival of music, theatre and dance.

7 Fort de Savoie, Colmars-les-Alpes

F2 04 92 83 41 92 Jun & Sep: 10am–noon Wed, Sat & Sun, 2–5:30pm Tue, Fri; Jul–Aug: 10am–noon & 2–6pm daily; other times by appt only

Perched atop medieval walls, this 17th-century fortress has a grim, business-like look when compared with the fairy-tale medieval castles found elsewhere in Provence. It was built to withstand cannon fire, not just arrows and siege towers. The work of master military engineer Vauban, it is a testimony to his skill. The Fort de France, the second of this former frontier garrison's strongholds, lies in ruins.

NAPOLEON AT SISTERON

On 1 March 1815, Napoleon Bonaparte escaped from exile on Elba and landed at Golfe Juan. Had the citadel at Sisteron been garrisoned by Royalist troops, his attempt to regain his Imperial throne might have been foiled, but he entered the town unopposed on 5 March to begin a triumphal progress to Paris, only to meet his final defeat at Waterloo.

8 Forcalquier

D3

This old town was once the seat of powerful local lords and the capital of the region. One gate of the old walled town, the Porte des Cordeliers, still survives, along with the restored cloisters and stark library of the 13th-century Couvent des Cordeliers *(blvd des Martyrs)*. The convent houses the tombs of the town's medieval *seigneurs* and is also home to the Artemisia Museum *(artemisia-museum.fr)*, which celebrates the region's aromatic and medicinal plants. Note, an entry fee is required to access the site.

9 Musée de Préhistoire des Gorges du Verdon

E3 Rte de Montmeyan, 04500 Quinson Feb–Mar & Oct–mid-Dec: 10am–6pm Wed–Mon (Apr–Jun & Sep: to 7pm); Jul, Aug: 10am–8pm daily Mid-Dec–Jan museeprehistoire.com

This museum, in a building designed by British architect Norman Foster, traces the geological, cultural and environmental evolution of human life in the Verdon and throughout Europe, with

Citadelle de Sisteron overlooking the town

a fascinating series of displays and interactive exhibits. Guided tours visit caves where relics of early humans have been found; call ahead to book.

10 Parc Naturel Régional du Verdon

E3–F3

Along the river Verdon, this regional park is a huge patchwork of landscapes, ranging from the neatly cultivated lavender fields of the sunlit Valensole plateau to the forested hills and pastures of the Artuby, the awesome chasms of the Gorges du Verdon *(p24)* and the beginnings of the Alps. There are brilliant blue lakes created where the Verdon has been dammed. This is a paradise for hikers, with a network of 700 km (450 miles) of paths, bridleways and ancient mule highways.

Canoeing in the Parc Naturel Régional du Verdon

A DRIVE THROUGH THE GORGES DU VERDON

Start after breakfast from the market town of **Castellane** *(p126)*, gateway to the canyons, and drive west on the D952. The landscape becomes progressively more awe-inspiring as you enter the gorges and wind your way through towering walls of rock to **Point Sublime** *(p25)*. This is one of the best viewpoints on the tour; savour it while enjoying a coffee or a cold drink at the pleasant **Auberge du Point Sublime** *(p127)*.

From here, drive for about 15 minutes and turn left on to the vertiginous **route des Crêtes** *(p25)*, which winds past a series of ever-higher viewpoints. Stop at each viewpoint for a few minutes, as the views keep varying. Finally, the road swings around the shoulder of the massif, and far below is the Verdon and the plateau country around the little village of **La Palud-sur-Verdon** *(p126)*. It takes another 30 minutes to reach, so relax at a café once you arrive.

When you are ready to set off again from La Palud, you'll find it a less daunting drive until the turquoise waters of the **Lac de Ste-Croix** *(p24)* come into sight. The road runs high above the lake, bringing you to the pretty village of **Moustiers-Sainte-Marie** *(p123)*. Reward yourself with lunch here, since the village happens to have one of the region's best restaurant, the excellent **Ferme Ste-Cécile** *(p127)*.

Towns and Villages

1. Seyne-les-Alpes

E2

Military and religious buildings are scattered through this quiet mountain town: a 15th-century gate, a medieval church and a ruined citadel are the main points of interest.

2. Les Mées

E3

The village of Les Mées is known for its Pénitents des Mées rock formations. Legend says these pinnacles were monks who broke their vows of chastity and were turned to stone by St Donat.

3. Simiane-la-Rotonde

D3

The enigmatic Rotonde, a Roman relic, whose purpose is still a puzzle, crowns the village to which it lends its name, a cluster of old houses and churches, as well as a ramshackle medieval fort.

4. Annot

F3

Annot stands in unspoiled countryside in the Vaïre valley. Many houses are built into the giant sandstone glacial boulders, known as the *grès d'Annot* – some have 17th- and 18th-century carved façades.

5. La Palud-sur-Verdon

E3

La Palud stands on the north side of the Gorges du Verdon, making it a very popular base for exploring the region.

6. Castellane

F3

Castellane is a lively market town surrounded by steep mountains. The Verdon flows through it, and it is a centre for adventure sports.

7. Allemagne-en-Provence

E3

Allemagne-en-Provence lies between the rugged canyon country of the Verdon and the lavender fields of the Valensole plateau. It is dominated by the splendidly palatial 12th-century Château d'Allemagne.

8. St-André-les-Alpes

F3

This little village bustles in summer. Built where the Verdon and Issole rivers flow into the human-made Lac de Castillon, it is a popular watersports centre, with dinghies, windsurfers and canoes for hire.

9. Beauvezer

F2

Beauvezer, in the dramatic Vallée du Haut Verdon, stands 1,179 m (3,600 ft) above sea level. It enjoys a pristine natural setting, near two major ski resorts (Le Seignus and La Foux).

10. Barcelonnette

F2

Provence's northernmost town is in the rugged Ubaye valley. As a result of 19th-century immigration, its architecture and festivals have a Mexican flavour. Rooftops may see a dusting of snow as late as June.

Simiane-la-Rotonde, fronted by a lavender field

Places to Eat

PRICE CATEGORIES

For a three-course meal for one with half a bottle of wine (or equivalent meal), taxes and extra charges.

€ under €40 **€€** €40–€60 **€€€** over €60

1. Le Grand Paris, Digne-les-Bains

E2 Hôtel du Grand Paris, 19 blvd Thiers L Tue–Wed, Dec–Mar hotel-grand-paris.com · €€€

This restaurant at Digne's best hotel serves classic dishes with a twist and offers exceptional service.

2. L'Auberge du Bois, Niozelles

D3 191 rte de Niozelles Oct–Mar laubergedubois.com · €€

This unpretentious inn specializes in Mediterranean dishes and offers terrace seating – tables are arranged around a small fountain and shaded by pine trees.

3. La Cantine, Moustiers-Sainte-Marie

E3 Rue de la Bourgade 04 92 77 46 64 Thu L & Sun · €€

Savour seasonal, locally sourced produce at La Cantine, whose menu offers meat, fish and vegetarian options. It's got a pretty outdoor dining area, too.

4. Kako Bistrot, Moustiers-Sainte-Marie

E3 Rue du Docteur Sénes L kakobistrot.com · €

A quirky little wine bar, Kako Bistrot is filled with retro paraphernalia ranging from mannequins to old phones.

5. Auberge du Point Sublime, Rougon

E3 Point Sublime Mid-Oct–Apr auberge-pointsublime.com · €

The location alone would make this inn special, with a terrace gazing out at the peaks of the Gorges du Verdon, but the local, traditional food is also sublime.

Outdoor area at La Cantine, Moustiers-Sainte-Marie

6. Ferme Ste-Cécile, Moustiers-Sainte-Marie

E3 Rte des Gorges du Verdon ferme-ste-cecile.com · €€

Catherine and Patrick Crespin serve contemporary food in an 18th-century farmhouse just outside the centre.

7. Le Jardin de Célina, Valensole

E3 Ancien chemin d'Allemagne Wed, Mon–Thu L lejardindecelina.com · €€

Set in the Parc Naturel Régional du Verdon, this spot offers modern dishes featuring Valensole produce.

8. La Caverne, Gréoux-les-Bains

E3 15 rue Grande Mon, Tue restaurant-lacaverne.com · €€

La Caverne may be small, but it is one of the best places in town for superb seafood and succulent Sisteron lamb.

9. Le Canap', Sisteron

E2 217 rue Droite Wed & Thu lecanap-sisteron.fr · €€

Founded by four childhood friends, this cosy French restaurant serves dishes made with local ingredients.

10. Le Tivoli, Sisteron

E2 21 pl Réné Cassin Wed, Thu L hoteltivoli-sisteron.fr · €€

The top-notch meat and fish dishes served at this small restaurant have made it a must-go place in town.

VAUCLUSE

Sitting in Provence's northwest, the Vaucluse département stretches from the orange and crimson canyons of the Parc Naturel Régional du Luberon in the south to the pretty peaks of Les Dentelles de Montmirail and the lonely summit of Mont Ventoux in the north. Such terrain makes the region a hub for outdoor pursuits, including cycling and hiking. There's plenty more to discover here, though, including Roman relics like the Théâtre Antique d'Orange and Vaison-la-Romaine, one of the finest Roman towns in Provence.

1 Vaison-la-Romaine

This craggy town has a medieval centre straddling the Ouvèze river *(p36)*. Its Roman archaeological site is one of the largest in the country.

2 Abbaye Notre-Dame de Sénanque

Surrounded by lavender fields, this medieval abbey *(p38)* is a pretty sight in summer, when the flowers bloom.

For places to stay in this area, see p149

Road winding its way up to the top of Mont Ventoux

3 Mont Ventoux

C2

The bald-headed "Giant of Provence" is the Vaucluse's greatest landmark; one that has inspired poets, mystics and botanists for centuries. Rising 1,910 m (6,260 ft), it commands the surrounding landscape, affording astonishing views to the sea, the Alps and the Rhône. Snowcapped in winter, the summit is revealed as arid chalk in summer and buffeted by strong winds all year round. The lower slopes are dense with trees, 1,000 plant varieties and wildlife.

4 Théâtre Antique d'Orange

B2 Rue Madeline Roch
Apr–Sep: 9am–6pm daily (Jun–Aug: to 7pm); Oct–Mar: 9:30am–4:30pm (Mar & Oct: to 5:30pm)
theatre-antique.com

The finest Roman theatre in Europe has its original stage wall, ensuring perfect acoustics.

5 Parc Naturel Régional du Luberon

C3 Maison du Parc, 60 pl Jean-Jaurès, Apt 8:30am–noon & 1:30–6pm Mon–Fri (Easter–Sep: also Sat am)

The Luberon has an untamed beauty. Covering 1,500 sq km (600 sq miles), it takes in the Petit Luberon of crags, gorges and perched villages to the west and the more rounded Grand Luberon to the east. The park's headquarters have information on walks, the ecology and the area's traditions.

Ochre cliffs in the Parc Naturel Régional du Luberon

6 Fontaine-de-Vaucluse
C3

From the base of 230-m- (750-ft-) high cliffs, Europe's most powerful spring pumps out the water that creates the River Sorgue. This natural wonder draws millions of visitors each year, just as it once attracted the 14th-century Italian poet Pétrarch. Downstream, the village celebrates its most famous resident with the Pétrarch Library Museum *(Rive gauche de la Sorgue)*, situated in one of the houses he is said to have lived in. The village also has two other excellent museums on chemin de la Fontaine: the Musée d'Histoire Jean Garcin: 1939–45, dedicated to World War II, and Le Monde Souterrain *(moulin-vallisclausa.com)*, which focuses on speleology.

7 Gorges de la Nesque
C3

The Gorges de la Nesque run for 20 km (12 miles) between the villages of Villes-sur-Auzon and Monieux. The rocky drop descends more than 300 m (1,000 ft), its sides bare or covered in scrub. Cut into the cliff, the winding road is definitely not for vertigo sufferers. The Castelleras viewpoint looks onto the Rocher du Cire (Wax Rock – so-called because of a local legend claiming that it is home to millions of bees). This is also the start of a testing walk to the bottom of the gorges, where Chapelle St-Michel is dug into the rock.

8 Les Dentelles de Montmirail
C2

Probably the prettiest mountain range in Provence, the Dentelles are formed by three ridges of chalk topped by ragged crests. The French think of these as lacework *(dentelles)*, but they can look more like fangs in rough weather. Within the range, tiny villages (Suzette, La Roque Alric) cling to the crags as if by magic and climbers are attracted to the sheer rock faces. The walking, too, is spectacularly good, notably up to St-Amand, at 730 m (2,400 ft), the highest point. Round the western edge cluster the picturesque wine villages of Beaumes-de-Venise, Gigondas, Vacqueyras and Séguret *(p133)*. There are marked wine routes through this picturesque vineyard region *(p70)*, and plenty of opportunities for tastings en route, but be sure to decide on a designated driver before you set off.

9 Avignon
B3

Situated along the Rhône, Avignon is known for its beautifully preserved medieval centre. Its main attraction is the magnificent Palais des Papes *(p22)*, a papal palace dating back to the 14th century. Other notable sights include

THE VAUDOIS MASSACRE

The bloodiest tale in Provençal history took place in Vaucluse in 1545, when Catholic Royal authorities determined to exterminate early Protestant settlers, the Vaudois. Within weeks, as many as 3,000 were dead: women and children were burned alive and villages were destroyed. The memories, and ruins, still haunt the remoter mountainsides.

Picturesque riverside village of Fontaine-de-Vaucluse

the pretty Cathédrale Notre-Dame-des-Doms *(p132)* and the art-filled Musée Calvet *(p132)*. The city is also famed for the summer Avignon Festival *(p74)*, which takes over the Palais des Papes' Court of Honour and other venues for both modern and classical drama. There's also an unofficial "off" festival, featuring street performers and up to 400 shows a day, ranging from dance to burlesque comedy.

10 Synagogue, Carpentras

C3 Pl Maurice Charretier 04 90 63 39 97 During religious services

Expelled from France in the 14th century, the Jews sought refuge in parts of Provence then belonging to the pope. This included Carpentras, whose synagogue, founded in 1367, is the oldest still functioning on French soil. Rebuilt in the 18th century, the synagogue looks like neighbouring buildings from the outside: laws forbade decoration. Within, a monumental staircase leads to the sumptuous two-storey area of worship (men upstairs, women below), and the setting for the tabernacle, teba, candelabra and chandeliers. Note, the synagogue offers guided tours on weekdays; call ahead to book.

The interior of the Synagogue in Carpentras

A DAY'S DRIVE IN THE VAUCLUSE MOUNTAINS

Morning

Start in Carpentras by visiting the **Synagogue**. Take the D942 to the **Gorges de la Nesque** to experience 20 km (12 miles) of awe-inspiring scenery. Pause at the Belvédère de Castelleras for breathtaking views.

Continue to Monieux, stopping at **Les Lavandes** restaurant *(restaurant-les-lavandes.fr)* in the village centre if it is time for lunch and you fancy elegant, classic cooking. Continue to **Sault** *(p53)* where, in July and August, the valley is a riot of purple lavender, yellow broom and the white of the rocks – an unmissable sight.

Afternoon

Take the D164 towards **Mont Ventoux** *(p129)*, another challenging drive, and stop for a break at the **Col des Tempêtes**. Take in the amazing views across the Toulourenc Valley, then journey to the summit for the most stunning panorama in Provence. Descend the mountain to **Malaucène** *(p133)*, taking the tiny D90 into the **Dentelles de Montmirail**. Pause in any of the cafés in **Beaumes-de-Venise** for a glass of the local sweet white wine. Continue to **Séguret** *(p133)* to roam its medieval streets, then return by the D7 to Carpentras, rewarding yourself with a delicious dinner at **Chez Serge** *(p135)*.

Avignon Sights

Ancient Pont d'Avignon over the Rhône

1. Place de l'Horloge

B3

Built on the old forum, the city's nerve centre is fringed with restaurants, bars and the 19th-century town hall.

2. Musée Angladon-Collection Jacques Doucet

B3 5 rue Laboureur Apr–Oct: 1–6pm Tue–Sun; Nov–Mar: 1–6pm Tue–Sat 1 Jan, 25 Dec angladon.com

This private collection includes fabulous works by Cézanne, Manet, Picasso and Van Gogh.

3. Rue des Teinturiers

B3

This tiny street – formerly home to dye-workers – now buzzes with arty cafés and quirky boutiques.

4. Palais des Papes

Dominating the city, this medieval papal palace *(p22)* stands as a symbol of Avignon's rich history.

5. Pont d'Avignon

B3 Blvd de la Ligne Daily; Mar: 9am–6:30pm; Apr–Jun & Sep–Oct: 9am–7pm (to 8pm Jul, to 8:30pm Aug); Nov–Feb: 9:30am–5:45pm

This 12th-century bridge, which originally had 22 arches, now has only four remaining.

6. Cathédrale Notre-Dame-des-Doms

B3 Pl du Palais metropole.diocese-avignon.fr

The medieval popes' cathedral has 17th-century alterations but a 13th-century altar.

7. Musée du Petit Palais

B3 Pl du Palais 04 90 86 44 58 10am–1pm, 2–6pm Wed–Mon 1 Jan, 1 May, 25 Dec

This superb collection of medieval and Renaissance art includes an early painting by Botticelli.

8. Collection Lambert

B3 Musée d'Art Contemporain, 5 rue Violette Hours vary, check website collectionlambert.com

This is Avignon's leading venue for contemporary art, featuring an array of thought-provoking exhibitions.

9. Chartreuse du Val-de-Bénédiction

B3 58 rue de la République, Villeneuve-lès-Avignon Hours vary, check website chartreuse.org

An impressive monastery and chapel with well-maintained, elegant gardens, perfect for peaceful strolls.

10. Musée Calvet

B3 65 rue Joseph Vernet 10am–1pm, 2–6pm Wed–Mon 1 Jan, 1 May, 25 Dec institutcalvet.fr

The Calvet is a fine museum, with collections of paintings, sculptures and artifacts from ancient Greece to the 20th century.

Sculpture of George Cuvier at Musée Calvet

Spectacularly sited medieval village of Gordes

Vaucluse Villages

1. Séguret

C2

This remarkably pretty medieval settlement hugs the hillside like a tight belt, offering gorgeous views.

2. Gordes

C3 gordes-village.com

Fashionable folk flock here, and no wonder. The village is perched above the Coulon Valley, and its little houses appear piled on top of one another. In the centre, the château oversees the whole with a stately Renaissance dignity.

3. Oppède-le-Vieux

C3

Flourishing in Renaissance times, Oppède was deserted by 1900 – no one wanted to live on a barely accessible rock. Now its houses are being restored by creative types, such as artists and writers, but the spot remains profoundly atmospheric, with medieval castle ruins.

4. Brantes

C2

Overhanging the gorges 550 m (1,800 ft) below, Brantes stares across the Toulourenc Valley to Mont Ventoux *(p129)*. Its tiny paved streets and vaulted passages boast a chapel but no shops. It is particularly impressive in March, when the almond trees are in bloom.

5. Malaucène

C2

This was where Pope Clement V had his summer residence, and it remains a grand place of 17th- and 18th-century houses, fountains and avenues shaded by plane trees.

6. Vacqueyras

B2

Vacqueyras is one of Provence's most prestigious wine villages. Admire the 11th-century church with its elegant bell tower, then go to taste the wine.

7. Ansouis

C3

This village, with its labyrinthe of narrow streets, is made truly remarkable by its château *(chateauansouis.fr)*, built in the 1100s and lived in by the same family until the early 2000s. The vaulted rooms, salons, armoury and kitchens are extraordinary, as are the stately gardens.

8. Roussillon

C3

Ochre mining and erosion have fashioned the multicoloured earth into cliffs and fantastic shapes, creating a bewitching setting for a romantic perched village.

9. Ménerbes

C3

Ménerbes was superbly sited for defence. As a Protestant stronghold, it held out for five years during the 16th-century Wars of Religion. The position remains dramatic, but peace now reigns around the citadel and townhouses. The views are terrific.

10. Le Barroux

C2

This eagle's nest of a village has narrow streets leading steeply up to the splendid château at the top.

Shops in Vaucluse

1. Chocolaterie Bernard Castelain, Châteauneuf-du-Pape

B3 1745 rte de Sorgues
chocolat-castelain.fr

This warehouse is packed with a dazzling array of chocolate. Enter only if you have iron self-control.

2. Farmers' Market, Velleron

C3 Apr–Sep: from 6pm Mon–Sat; Oct–Mar: from 4:30pm Tue, Wed, Fri & Sat

In the Farmers' Market, held in the evening, stallholders sell home-grown or home-raised produce only.

3. Nougats Silvain, St-Didier

C3 4 pl Neuve nougats-silvain.fr

This is a farming and fruit-growing family known for their delicious nougat. Don't miss the honey, either.

4. Lou Canesteou, Vaison-la-Romaine

C2 10 rue Raspail
loucanesteou.com

Josiane Déal personally selects the 160 varieties of artisanal cheese for her shop, and has been named a *Meilleur Ouvrier* ("Master of her Craft") for her expertise.

5. Olivades, Avignon

B3 56 rue Joseph Vernet
olivades.fr

This company has been producing and printing Provençal fabrics since 1818. It's now the only such outfit in the region, with materials, table linen and wedding gowns.

Treats at Chocolaterie Bernard Castelain

6. Edith Mézard, Goult

C3 Château de l'Ange

The château near Goult features beautifully embroidered clothes and a great range of linen for the house.

7. Confiserie Artisanale Denis Ceccon, Apt

C3 24 quai de la Liberté
confiserie-saintdenis.fr

Apt is known for its crystallized fruit, and Denis Ceccon is one of the few artisans working by traditional methods – try the apricots.

8. Les Délices du Luberon, L'Isle-sur-la-Sorgue

C3 1 av du Partage des Eaux
delices-du-luberon.fr

A warehouse selling olives and olive products such as tapenade or *melet* (a mix of fennel, peppers, olives and anchovies).

9. Château Pesquié, Mormoiron

C2 1365 bis rte de Flassan
chateaupesquie.com

The Château Pesquié features lovely grounds and first-rate Ventoux wines.

10. L'Isle-sur-la-Sorgue

C3

Over 200 shops make this town France's top antiques centre after Paris. Most are open Saturday to Monday, with a market on Sunday mornings. Antiques fairs are held at Easter and around All Saints' Day.

Antique items on sale in L'Isle-sur-la-Sorgue

Places to Eat

1. La Fourchette, Avignon

B3 17 rue Racine Sat, Sun, 3 wks in Aug la-fourchette.eatbu.com • €€

A local favourite, this country-inn-style spot features Provençal classics, like sumptuous *boeuf en daube (p69)*.

2. Hiély Lucullus, Avignon

B3 5 rue de la République Tue, Wed hielly-lucullus.com • €€

One of Avignon's oldest restaurants, which adds a wonderful lightness of touch to its classic dishes.

3. Chez Serge, Carpentras

C3 90 rue Cottier chez-serge.fr • €€

Chef Serge's bistro is acclaimed for its good-value Provençal dishes. Its wine and truffle evenings are especially popular.

4. Restaurant Sevin, Avignon

B3 10 rue de Mons Wed, Thu restaurantsevin.fr • €€€

Tasting menus of superb Provençal fare are matched with excellent wines at this esteemed restaurant.

5. Auberge la Fenière, Lourmarin

C3 Rte de Lourmarin Hours vary, check website aubergelafeniere.com • €€

Nadia Sammut, one of France's rare female top chefs, brings international influence to regional cuisine.

6. Le Prieuré, Villeneuve-lès-Avignon

B3 7 pl du Chapitre Nov–Mar leprieure.com • €€€

The locally sourced menu changes four times a week, offering gourmet cuisine in a heavenly setting.

7. Les Florets, Gigondas

B2 1243 rte des Florêts Wed, Jan–mid-Mar hotel-lesflorets.com • €€

Dine on the terrace at Les Florets and savour regional cuisine paired with an excellent wine list, all while enjoying superb views of the Dentelles de Montmirail.

PRICE CATEGORIES

For a three-course meal for one with half a bottle of wine (or equivalent meal), taxes and extra charges.

€ under €40 **€€** €40–€60 **€€€** over €60

8. Hygge, Avignon

B3 25 pl des Carmes 04 86 34 55 70 Hours vary, call ahead • €

At Hygge, enjoy cantine-style cooking and natural wines. Relax on the patio, shaded by vines and parasols.

9. Le Moulin à Huile, Vaison-la-Romaine

C2 1 quai Maréchal Foch Tue, Wed lemoulinahuile84.fr • €€€

Superb setting in the medieval part of town. The chefs prepare excellent regional dishes for a set menu.

10. La Bastide de Capelongue, Bonnieux

C3 Les Claparèdes, chemin des Cabanes Hours vary, check website confiserie-saintdenis.fr • €€€

Chef Noël Bérard is known for aromatic Provençal cuisine, using his own herbs for dishes such as rack of lamb smoked with wild thyme.

Cosy interior of the Auberge la Fenière in Lourmarin

STREETSMART

Vintage car in Pays de Fayence

RUE
DROITE

GETTING AROUND

Whether you're visiting Provence and the Côte d'Azur for a short city break or rural country retreat, discover how best to reach your destination and travel around like a pro.

AT A GLANCE

AVIGNON

€1.40

(single bus journey)

MARSEILLE

€2

(single bus, metro or tram journey)

NICE

€1.50

(single bus journey)

TOP TIP

Avoid on-the-spot fines by stamping your ticket to validate your journey.

SPEED LIMITS

AUTOROUTES	DUAL CARRIAGEWAYS
130 **km/h** (80 mph)	**110** **km/h** (68 mph)

SINGLE CARRIAGEWAYS	URBAN AREAS
90 **km/h** (56 mph)	**30** **km/h** (18 mph)

Arriving by Air

Provence has five international airports in Avignon, Marseille, Nice, Nîmes and Toulon-Hyères; all are near their respective cities, with good bus services to the city centres.

Nice Airport is the main gateway for Provence, with frequent flights from Paris, London, New York and other major cities. Buses run the 7 km (4 miles) to central Nice every 15 minutes. Other direct airport buses regularly serve Antibes, Cannes and Monaco. It's also possible to take a taxi.

Marseille Airport is situated 25 km (16 miles) northwest of Marseille and 28 km (17 miles) southwest of Aix-en-Provence. Buses run to Marseille-St-Charles railway station about every 15 minutes, and numerous other direct buses serve Aix-en-Provence, St-Tropez and other cities and towns. Taxis are another option.

Avignon Airport is 10 km (6 miles) from the city centre; a taxi or LER bus takes 40 minutes. Nîmes Airport is 13 km (8 miles) from Nîmes; a taxi or Navette Aéroport coach to the city takes 15 minutes. Toulon-Hyères Airport is 24 km (15 miles) from Toulon and 8 km (5 miles) from Hyères; the Réseau Mistral bus takes 30 minutes and 20 minutes, respectively, to reach the city centres.

Monaco has no airport but has a city-centre heliport with a 7-minute **Héli Securité** shuttle service to Nice Airport.

Héli Securité
W helisecurite.fr

International Train Travel

High-speed TGV trains connect Provence with Italy, Spain and Switzerland. Most TGV stations are located in city centres except for Avignon and Aix-en-Provence, whose airport-style stations are a short bus ride from the city centre. Reservations for all TGV services are essential as tickets are booked up quickly. Visit the **RENFE-SNCF** or **OUI SNCF** websites for tickets, depending on your route. **Eurostar** services run directly from London to Avignon and Marseille.

You can buy tickets for multiple international journeys via **Eurail** or **Interrail**; you may need to pay additional reservation fees. Students and those under 26 and over 60 can benefit from discounted rail travel both to and within France.

Eurail
W eurail.com
Eurostar
W eurostar.com
Interrail
W interrail.eu
OUI-SNCF
W sncf-connect.com
RENFE-SNCF
W renfe.com

Regional and Local Trains

Every major town in Provence is connected by high-speed TGV trains, run by the French rail operator **SNCF**. Even tiny villages are linked by **TER**, also operated by SNCF, which serves every station on local and suburban routes.

Advance purchase is a good idea during the busy summer months, but is not essential at other times.

The historic narrow-gauge **Train des Pignes** is a popular journey. It runs from Nice's Gare de Provence to Digne-les-Bains in the Hautes-Alpes through splendid Alpine scenery. The **Train des Merveilles** is another great route, particularly for hikers. The line runs from Nice deep into the Italian Alps through what was Italian territory until 1947, past the towns of Tende and Sospel.

SNCF
W sncf.com
TER
W ter-sncf.com
Train des Merveilles
W ter.sncf.com
Train des Pignes
W traindespignes.fr

Long-Distance Bus Travel

BlaBlaCar coaches connect many cities in Provence with Paris, Lyon, Toulouse, Montpellier and Bordeaux. **Flixbus** connects cities in Provence with Paris, as well as with other French towns and major European destinations.

BlaBlaCar
W blablacar.fr/bus
Flixbus
W flixbus.fr

Driving to Provence

It takes ten hours to drive to Avignon from the Channel ferry ports via the A26 and A27 *autoroutes*. Driving from Bilbao in Spain – served by ferries from the UK – takes around eight hours. The drive from Paris to Provence is an easy one, except around French holidays. Allow at least six hours for the 700-km (435-mile) journey to Avignon via the A6 Autoroute du Soleil, as well as about €60 in tolls. Allow ten hours to Nice plus around €80 in tolls. There are *aires* (rest stops) every 30 km (20 miles) or so. Most have picnic tables and public toilets.

To take your own car into France, you will need proof of registration, valid insurance documents, a full, valid driving licence and your passport.

GETTING TO AND FROM THE AIRPORT

Airport	Distance to City	Taxi Fare	Public Transport	Journey Time
Avignon	10 km (6 miles)	€30–35	LER 13 bus	40 mins
Marseille	25 km (16 miles)	€70–85	L91 Navette Aéroport coach	25 mins
Nice	7 km (4 miles)	€35	Lignes d'Azur tram lines 2 and 3	20 mins
Nîmes	13 km (8 miles)	€25	Navette Aéroport coach	15 mins
Toulon-Hyères to Toulon	24 km (15 miles)	€65	102 Réseau Mistral bus	30 mins
Toulon-Hyères to Hyères	8 km (5 miles)	€22	63 Réseau Mistral bus	20 mins

Public Transport

Each urban area in Provence has a public transport system. Safety and hygiene measures, timetables, ticket information, transport maps and more can be found on their respective websites.

City Transport

The region's cities have efficient transport networks. **Orizo** is the local operator for Avignon and its suburbs, including the city's trams and its hop-on, hop-off electric shuttle buses. In Marseille, **RTM** co-ordinates bus, metro and tram lines, as well as ferries from the Vieux Port to Pointe-Rouge and l'Estaque. **CAM** operates buses within Monaco and to Nice and Menton, and a series of lifts and escalators connect its waterfront with the upper urban level. **Lignes d'Azur** is the operator for Nice, Cannes and Alpes-Maritimes, including the Nice tram system. **Réseau Mistral** is Toulon's city and suburban public bus and boat-bus network.

CAM
W cam.mc
Lignes d'Azur
W lignesdazur.com
Orizo
W orizo.fr
Réseau Mistral
W reseaumistral.com
RTM
W rtm.fr

Tickets

Buying tickets in advance is always cheaper than buying from the driver. *Carnets* (books of up to ten tickets) and multi-trip passes valid for one or more days are available on all urban transport networks and can be bought at rail and bus stations, designated stores and city tourist-information offices.

Local Buses

Beyond major towns, local bus routes are served by private companies under regional authority governance. Timetables are geared to the needs of local schools and shoppers, rather than visitors. **ZOU!** is the one-stop shop for local buses across the region.

ZOU!
W zou.maregionsud.fr

Taxis

There are taxi ranks at rail and bus stations, airports and in most main squares in towns and cities. You can also call or text for taxis.

Driving in Provence

Driving in Provence can be a pleasure, but plan your journey carefully to avoid traffic bottlenecks on rural and coastal roads in summer.

For a fast point-to-point journey, the A8 *autoroute* cuts across the Camargue from Menton to Aix-en-Provence, near which it meets the A7 Autoroute du Soleil, so you can drive on *autoroutes* all the way across Provence from the Italian border to Orange in just over three hours. The same journey avoiding *autoroutes* takes more than six hours but costs less, as the A8 is the most expensive toll road in France.

Routes départementales are the narrowest and slowest roads, but in hinterland regions such as Alpes-de-Hautes-Provence they may be your only option. **Bison Futé** signs indicate routes avoiding heavy traffic and can be useful during French holidays.

Driving in the historic centres of Provençal towns is not recommended, due to one-way streets and expensive parking. In summer, traffic on the coast road between Hyères and Nice, and especially the section between Nice and Cannes, is often very slow.

Bison Futé
W bison-fute.gouv.fr

Car Hire

To hire a car in France you must be 21 years or over and have held a valid driver's licence for at least a year. You will also need to present a credit card. Driving licences issued by any of the EU member states are valid throughout the EU. International driving licences are not needed for short-term visitors (up to 90 days) from the UK, North America, Australia and New Zealand. Visitors from other countries should check with their automobile association.

All the main car-hire companies have offices in Provençal towns. Nice has an all-electric car-share scheme: **Mobilize Share**.

Mobilize Share
W fr.share.mobilize.com

Rules of the Road

Always drive on the right. Unless otherwise signposted, vehicles coming from the right have right of way, as do cars on a roundabout.

At all times, drivers must carry a valid driver's licence, registration and insurance documents. In case of a breakdown, it is compulsory to carry a red warning triangle and a luminous vest. Seatbelts must be worn, and it is prohibited to sound your horn in cities except in a genuine emergency. For motorbikes and scooters, the wearing of helmets and protective gloves is compulsory. It is against the law to drive in urban bus lanes. France strictly enforces its drink-drive limit *(p145)*, and random breath testing at mobile checkpoints is common.

Parking

Park only in areas with a large "P" or a *Payant* sign on the pavement or road, and pay at the parking meter with cash or contactless. Avignon, Marseille, Nice and Toulon have numerous underground car parks, signposted by a white "P" on a blue background, and overground car parks are usually located on the edge of historic town centres.

Boats and Ferries

Boats are a great way to take a day trip along the coast. Most useful are the **Trans Côte d'Azur** ferries from Cannes to the Îles de Lérins, and **Bateaux Verts** from Ste-Maxime to St-Tropez. Boat tours are also run around Avignon and into the Camargue.

The free *navette fluviale* (river shuttle), also known as the *bac à traille*, crosses the Rhône between the Quai de la Ligne in central Avignon and Île de la Barthelasse. **Bateliers de la Côte d'Azur**, meanwhile, sail from Toulon to the Îles d'Hyères.

Bateau Verts
W bateauxverts.com
Bateliers de la Côte d'Azur
W bateliersdelacote dazur.com
Trans Côte d'Azur
W trans-cote-azur.com

Cycling

Bike rental in Provence is widely available. **Vélopop'** in Avignon, **Le Vélo** in Marseille and **Lime** in Nice are bike-sharing schemes; the latter also offers e-scooters. Register online first, and then grab a bike from one of the multiple docking stations around each city. Aix-en-Provence doesn't have a bike-sharing scheme, but **Aixprit Vélo** bike shop hires out bikes in the city.

Bicycles may be taken on most trains, but book in advance for TGV trains. To take your bike on a local train, look for the bicycle symbol on the timetable. Wearing a helmet is strongly advised.

Aixprit Vélo
W aixpritvelo.com
Le Vélo
W levelo.ampmetropole.fr
Lime
W li.me
Vélopop'
W velo-grandavignon.fr

Walking

Most cities in Provence are extremely walkable, with sights only a short distance apart. Outside urban areas, you'll find both *sentiers balisés* (local trails) and *sentiers de grande randonnée* (long-distance hiking tracks); both are part of a vast network that covers all of France. The main long-distance trails are the GR5, GR51, GR6 and GR9. Maps and guides are widely available from tourist offices.

PRACTICAL INFORMATION

A little local know-how goes a long way in Provence and the Côte d'Azur. On these pages you can find all the essential advice and information you will need to make the most of your trip to this region.

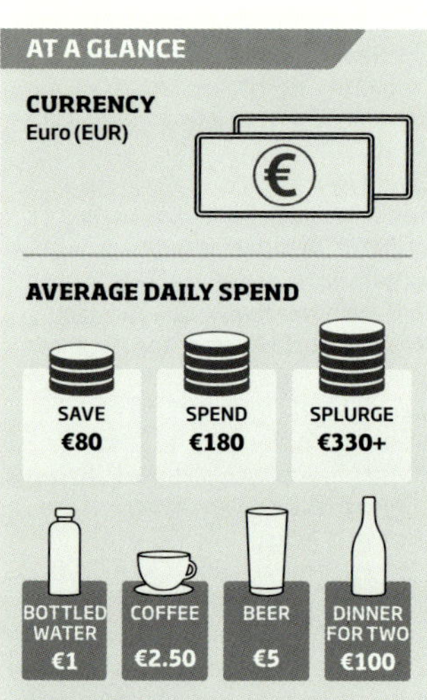

ESSENTIAL PHRASES

Hello	Bonjour
Thank you	Merci
Please	S'il vous plaît
Goodbye	Au revoir
Do you speak English?	Parlez-vous anglais?
I don't understand...	Je ne comprends pas...

ELECTRICITY SUPPLY

Power sockets are type C and E, fitting two-pronged plugs. Standard voltage is 230 volts.

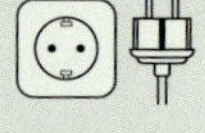

Passports and Visas

For entry requirements, including visas, consult your nearest French embassy or check the **France-Visas** website. Visitors from outside the European Economic Area (EEA), European Union (EU) and Switzerland need a valid passport to enter France. EEA, EU and Swiss nationals can use their national identity cards instead. Citizens of the UK, Canada, the US, Australia and New Zealand can visit France for up to three months but, from 2026, must apply in advance for the European Travel Information and Authorization System (**ETIAS**). Visitors from other countries may also require an ETIAS, so check before travelling. EU nationals do not need a visa or an ETIAS.

ETIAS
W etiasvisa.com
France-Visas
W france-visas.gouv.fr

Government Advice

Now more than ever, it is important to consult both your and the French government's advice before travelling. The **UK Foreign, Commonwealth and Development Office (FCDO)**, the **US Department of State**, the **Australian Department of Foreign Affairs and Trade** and **Gouvernement France** offer all the latest information on security, health and local regulations.

Australian Department of Foreign Affairs and Trade
W smarttraveller.gov.au
Gouvernement France
W gouvernement.fr
UK Foreign, Commonwealth and Development Office (FCDO)
W gov.uk/foreign-travel-advice
US Department of State
W travel.state.gov

Customs Information

You can find information on the laws relating to goods and currency taken

in or out of France on the **Douanes et Droits Indirects** website.
Douanes et Droits Indirects
W douane.gouv.fr

Insurance

We recommend that you take out a comprehensive insurance policy covering theft, loss of belongings, medical care, cancellations and delays, and read the small print carefully.

EU and UK citizens are eligible for free emergency medical care provided they have a valid European Health Insurance Card (EHIC) or a UK Global Health Insurance Card (**GHIC**). Visitors from outside the EU must arrange their own private medical insurance.
GHIC
W nhs.uk

Vaccinations

No innoculations are needed for France.

Money

Most establishments accept major credit, debit and pre-paid currency cards. Contactless payments are accepted in major cities. Most taxi drivers and market traders, as well as many smaller bars and restaurants, accept only cash, so do carry a small amount with you.

Tips are generally included as part of the bill in France, although some locals will tip extra for exceptional service (around 5–10 per cent of the total bill). Hotel porters and housekeeping generally expect a tip of €1 to €2 per bag or day. For taxi journeys, round up the fare to the nearest euro.

Travellers with Specific Requirements

Most museums in Provence are wheelchair-accessible and offer audio tours and induction loops. **Disabled Holidays** specializes in accommodation for travellers with specific requirements. Fully supported activity holidays are offered by **Go Beyond**.

To find out about accessible public transport and attractions in Nice, visit the **Nice Tourisme** website. For Marseille, the **Marseille Tourisme** website offers useful information for travellers with specific requirements. National train operator SNCF offers **Accès Plus**, which accompanies travellers with specific requirements on rail journeys.
Accès Plus
W sncf-connect.com/accessibilite
Disabled Holidays
W disabledholidays.com
Go Beyond
W gobeyondholidays.com
Nice Tourisme
W explorenicecotedazur.com
Marseille Tourisme
W marseille-tourisme.com

Language

French is the official language spoken in France. English is spoken in large hotels, but not in all smaller establishments, shops, bars and cafés, so mastering a few niceties goes a long way.

Opening Hours

In general, big stores and supermarkets open from 8am to 7pm, plus 9am to 1pm on Sundays. Many smaller shops and businesses close for an hour or two from around noon and are closed on Sundays and public holidays. Very few restaurants serve lunch after 2pm.

Museums have similar opening hours across the entire region. Almost all of them are open from 10am to 6pm Tuesday to Sunday. Outdoor cultural sights often stay open later in summer.

Situations can change quickly and unexpectedly. Always check before visiting attractions and hospitality venues for up-to-date opening hours and booking requirements.

Personal Security

Provence is generally a safe region, though petty crime can take place. Beware of bag-snatchers and pick-pockets on public transport, especially during rush hour and in major tourist areas. Use your common sense and be alert to your surroundings, and you should have a trouble-free trip. If you have anything stolen, report the crime to the nearest police station, and bring ID. Get a copy of the crime report in order to claim on your insurance. Contact your embassy or consulate if your passport is stolen, or in the event of a serious crime or accident.

Like the rest of France, Provence is diverse and multicultural. As a rule, Provençals are accepting of all people regardless of their race, gender or sexuality, although rural Provence tends to be more conservative than the big cities. Same-sex marriage was legalized in 2013, and France recognized the right to legally change your gender in 2016. Nice, Cannes, Aix-en-Provence and especially Marseille have thriving LGBTQ+ communities.

AT A GLANCE

EMERGENCY NUMBERS

GENERAL EMERGENCY	FIRE SERVICE AND AMBULANCE
112	**18**

POLICE	MEDICAL EMERGENCY
17	**15**

TIME ZONE
CET/CEST
Central European Summer Time (CEST); last Sun Mar–last Sun Oct.

TAP WATER
Unless stated otherwise, tap water in France is safe to drink.

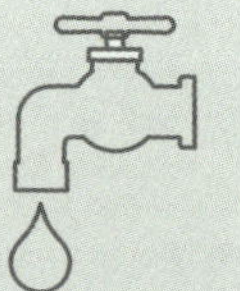

WEBSITES AND APPS

Bison Futé
Official road-journey website and app *(bison-fute.gouv.fr)*.

SNCF Connect
Buy and download rail tickets direct to your phone or tablet with this app.

PACA Mobilité
Official app for public transport through the Provence-Alpes-Côte d'Azur area.

ViaMichelin
App for road-travel planning, including journey times and traffic information.

Health

France has a world-class healthcare system. Emergency medical care is free for all UK and EU nationals. If you have an EHIC or GHIC *(p143)*, present this as soon as possible. You may have to pay for treatment and reclaim the money later. For other visitors, payment of medical expenses is the patient's responsibility, so arrange comprehensive medical insurance before travelling.

A green cross indicates a pharmacy; these are an excellent source of advice – they can diagnose many health problems and suggest treatment. Call 3237 to find the nearest pharmacy. They are usually open from 9am to 8pm Monday to Saturday. When closed, there will be a sign in the window giving the location of the nearest *pharmacie de nuit*, which will be open. If you need to visit a doctor, book an appointment with **Doctolib**.

Provence has its share of pests, from mosquitoes to jellyfish; beware of spiky sea urchins if walking on rocky shores.

Doctolib
doctolib.fr

Smoking, Alcohol and Drugs

Smoking is prohibited in all public places, but is allowed on open-air restaurant, café and bar terraces. The possession of illegal drugs is prohibited and could result in a prison sentence. Unless stated otherwise, alcohol consumption on the streets is permitted. France has a strict limit of 0.05 per cent BAC (blood alcohol content) for drivers.

ID

There is no requirement for visitors to carry ID, but in the event of a routine check you may be asked to show your passport. If you don't have it with you, the police may escort you to wherever your passport is being kept.

Local Customs

Étiquette *(la politesse)* is important in France. Upon entering a store or café say *bonjour* and, when leaving, say *au revoir*. Be sure to add *s'il vous plaît* (please) when ordering and *pardon* (sorry) if you accidentally bump into someone.

The French usually shake hands when meeting someone for the first time. Friends and colleagues may greet each other with a kiss on each cheek.

When visiting churches and cathedrals, dress respectfully and keep mobile phones on silent.

Responsible Travel

There are several ways to travel more responsibly in Provence, including by making use of public transport *(p140)* and city bike-share schemes *(p141)*. At the beach, use reef-safe sunscreen to protect marine life and, when hiking, stay on marked trails to avoid damaging flora. Due to climate change, there's more risk of drought and wildfires; conserve water by taking showers instead of baths and reusing hotel towels.

Mobile Phones and Wi-Fi

Free Wi-Fi hotspots are available in a number of public spaces, including museums, libraries and parks. Most hotels and many cafés and restaurants offer free Wi-Fi for patrons.

Visitors with EU mobile phone contracts can use their devices in Provence without additional charges. Those not on EU tariffs should check roaming rates with their provider.

Mobile phone coverage in most cities, towns and villages is good but mobile and GPS reception in some mountainous areas is patchy.

Post

Post offices, *tabacs* (tobacconists) and **La Poste** website sell stamps *(timbres)*. Most post offices have self-service machines to weigh and frank your mail. Yellow post boxes are ubiquitous.

La Poste
W laposte.fr

Taxes and Refunds

A sales tax (TVA) of 20 per cent is imposed on most goods and services. Non-EU residents can reclaim the TVA they pay on French goods at shops displaying the Global Refund Tax-Free sign as long as they spend more than €175 in the same shop in one day, and take the goods out of France. The retailer will generally supply a form and issue a *détaxe* receipt at the time of purchase. Make sure that you have your passport with you to prove non-resident status.

Discount Cards

City and regional passes can help you cut the cost of sightseeing and public transport. The **Avignon City Pass** offers free access to museums, monuments and gardens in Avignon and Villeneuve-lès-Avignon, as well as official themed guided tours. The **French Riviera Pass** allows free access to many sights, tours and activities, and free travel on public transport throughout the Nice-Côte d'Azur metropolitan area. The **Marseille CityPass** includes free public transport, free admission to museums and galleries and other discounts.

Avignon City Pass
W avignon-citypass.com
French Riviera Pass
W en.frenchrivierapass.com
Marseille CityPass
W marseille-tourisme.com

PLACES TO STAY

Provence's accommodation is as varied as its landscape. Along the coast, flashy five-star properties with palatial suites rub shoulders with toes-in-the-sand campsites, a mere hop from the sea. Inland, choose from a selection of homestays, treehouses, wineries and more.

The summer holidays (Jul & Aug) are high season in much of Provence, when rates hike and occupancy swells, although Luberon sees an early spike from mid-June to mid-July to coincide with the lavender bloom.

PRICE CATEGORIES

For a standard, double room per night (with breakfast if included), taxes and extra charges.

€ under €200
€€ €200–€400
€€€ over €400

Marseille

Grande Juste

M5 80 rue Auguste Blanqui justejuste.com · €

Most key sights are within walking distance of this design hotel, housed in a renovated 19th-century convent and found just 15 minutes on foot from the Vieux Port. Grand Juste is eco-friendly, too: it's Green Key certified; its furniture and décor are second-hand; and its tasty breakfasts – served until 1pm – are made with fresh, local produce.

Hotel 96

C5 96 av de la Soude hotel96.com · €

Light, bright and enclosed by greenery, this well-run spot is for those who don't want to choose between the city and the beach. It's located between Marseille and the *calanques*, with buses running to both the city centre and Prado Beach. And if you don't fancy straying far, there's a tree-lined swimming pool to relax by.

Pitchounette et Olives

J6 11 blvd Tellene pitchounetteetolives.com · €

Run by a friendly couple, this cosy spot – offering just three rooms – feels like a welcoming home from home. You'll need to share a bathroom, but at this price, you won't mind – especially when the rate includes a welcome drink and breakfast.

The People

K3 7 rue Jean-Marc Cathala thepeoplehostel.com · €

The rainbow-hued walls at this centrally located hostel are reminiscent of Marseille's most vibrant street, cours Julien. Choose from 4- to 8-bed dorms and double rooms, and expect a super-social vibe, with free welcome drinks that help get conversation flowing.

Casa Youm

C5 12 plt du Peintre casayoum.com · €€

Casa Youm could have stepped out of a boho interior-design magazine; think bamboo towel racks and earthenware sinks in the bathrooms. It's the perfect place to kick back: do yoga overlooking the sea, sunbathe poolside or take in the sea views.

Bouches-du-Rhône

La Bulle du Lavandin

D4 4380 rte de St-Canadet, Aix-en-Provence labulledulavandin.fr · €

Perched next to a lavender field, this semi-transparent "bubble" tent is a joy to sleep in. During the day, there are views over the lavender fields, which bloom in summer, while at night the sky above will blaze with stars. Facilities include a dry toilet and alfresco shower.

Lodge Sainte Hélène

A4 273 chemin Bas des Launes, Saintes-Maries-de-la-Mer lodge-saintehelene.com · €€

Found on the edge of the Camargue, this beautiful collection of whitewashed lodges offers stunning views over the delta's waters and wildlife; each lodge has a private patio from where you can soak them in. If you want to explore the delta, the lodge offers bicycle hire (regular or electric) and activities such as horse riding.

L'Hotel Particulier Arles

B4 4 rue de la Monnaie, Arles hotel-particulier.com · €€€

This handsome manor house offers a taste of French luxury. Built in the early 19th century for the mayor of Arles, its 10 rooms retain plenty of period features, with gilded furniture and wood-panelled walls. Its facilities, though, are decidedly 21st century: highlights include a vaulted spa and heated pool in the leafy garden.

The Var and Provençal Coast

Les Cabanes du Varon

F4 3029 rte de Salernes, Flayosc cabanesduvaron.com · €

Looking for something a little more offbeat? Les Cabanes du Varon won't disappoint. Choose from lodgings in a cute treehouse with Star Wars-style Ewok vibes or a cosy hobbit hole named after a *Lord of the Rings* character. Not quite quirky enough? Each hobbit hole has an escape game to play.

Château de Berne

F4 chemin des Imberts, Flayosc chateauberne.com · €€€

Wine lovers rejoice: this opulent property is ringed by swathes of organic vineyards. Sample a glass of the good stuff in its Michelin-starred restaurant, which offers dishes made with produce from the estate and surrounding area, or take a tour of the château's vast wine cellar. Even if you're not into wine, there's lots to draw you here, whether that's taking a stroll through the estate's beautiful grounds or simply chilling out by the pool in the tiered garden.

Lou Calen

E4 1 cours Gambetta, Cotignac loucalen.com · €€€

This rustic-yet-chic hotel has more experiences than you can shake a stick at, from laid-back offerings like water-colour workshops to more active options such as truffle-hunting with the hotel's friendly dogs. There's so much to do that there's little need to leave the hotel, but make time to venture out; on the hotel's doorstep are goat tracks through olive groves and charming, lost-in-time Provençal villages.

MUSE St-Tropez

F5 364 chemin de Val de Rian, Ramatuelle muse-hotels.com · €€€

Nature reigns supreme at this boutique property in the hills outside St-Tropez, with 16 suites framed by pines and palms. Inside, the muted tones of the décor reflect the leafy location and – in a nod to the hotel's name – each of the suites are named after inspirational women, such as Colette and Édith Piaf.

Nice

Hostel Meyerbeer Beach

P5 15 rue Meyerbeer hostelmeyerbeer.com · €

This cheap-and-cheerful hostel is a good option for those watching their money. The beach is only a street away, and the hostel organizes free walking tours and bar crawls. There's a good mix of room types, too, with 4- to 8-person dormitories and double, triple and quad rooms on offer.

Mama Shelter Nice

R4 21 blvd de Riquier mamashelter.com · €

This outpost of Mama Shelter – somewhat of a national phenomenon – has the usual kitsch and colourful vibe, with patterned furnishings, bright tiles and abstract ceiling murals. Don't miss the spectacular rooftop terrace, with its beautiful tiled pool. It won't break the bank, either.

Hôtel du Couvent

R4 1 rue Honoré Ugo
hotelducouvent.com
· €€€

This renovated 18th-century convent is a peaceful oasis in the heart of bustling Vieux Nice. The minimalistic rooms – complete with plaster-hued walls and soft pink tiles – honour the convent's original character without feeling too austere. But it's the outdoor spaces that steal the show, including a terraced garden overlooking the Mediterranean.

Monaco and the Riviera

Hotel les Roches Rouges

G5 90 blvd de la 36ème division du Texas, St-Raphaël
beaumier.com · €€€

Set by the beach on the edge of Cap Estérel, this Modernist-style hotel is famed for its panoramic sea views. Take them in from the stylish rooms, or head down to the two pools (freshwater and saltwater) that practically rub noses with the sea. The hotel is found in one of the most unspoilt parts of the Riviera, so there are plenty of outdoor activities on the doorstep.

Hotel Lemon, Menton

H3 10 rue Albert 1er, Menton hotel-lemon.fr
· €

This little place packs a punch, with spacious, handsomely designed rooms, and a courtyard patio for enjoying breakfast in the shade of lemon trees. The location is great, too: a short walk from both the town centre and the beach. The only downside? There's no lift, so top-floor rooms can be a struggle if you have heavy luggage.

Hotel Barrière le Majestic, Cannes

G4 10 blvd de la Croisette, Cannes
hotelsbarriere.com/cannes/le-majestic
· €€€

Not one for blending in, this huge and historic hotel dominates Cannes' waterfront. Expect facilities that are all singing, all dancing, including two restaurants, two bars, a spa, a pool and a cinema. There's even a private beach.

Alpes-Maritimes

Toile Blanche

G4 826 chemin de la Pounchounière, St-Paul-de-Vence
toileblanche.com · €€€

An artistic haven, Toile Blanche was set up by artists collective Leroy Brothers in St-Paul-de-Vence, a pretty village that has long attracted creative types. The hotel's name, meaning "blank canvas", aptly sums up the 22 gallery-like suites, with art hung tastefully around the minimalist rooms. The hotel hosts regular exhibitions, too.

Camping Domaine de la Bergerie

F5 1960 rte Départementale 8, quartier du Fournel, Roquebrune-sur-Argens camping-domainedelabergerie.com · €

Get back to nature at this friendly campsite, which has been run by the same family for over 70 years. Camping and caravanning spots are nestled beneath leafy trees, with a huge area of forest to explore nearby. The facilities are excellent, with two swimming pools, *pétanque* grounds and a grocer's shop stocking local goods.

Hotel le Druos

G2 Front de Neige, Isola 2000 hoteldruos.com · €

Don't judge a book by its cover: Hotel le Druos might look bland from the outside, but inside it's all polished wood and Alpine charm, with rooms that look right over the mountains. The location isn't bad, either: right in the heart of Isola 2000's ski station, with direct access to the pistes.

Hotel du Cap-Eden-Roc

G4 167-165 blvd J F Kennedy, Antibes
oethercollection · €€€

It would be easier to come up with a list of celebrities who haven't stayed at this hotel, as it's been welcoming the rich and famous since 1870. Everyone from Elizabeth Taylor to Heidi Klum has been lured by its classic rooms, gorgeous Dior spa and infinity pool that hangs over the Mediterranean.

Le 1932 Hotel & Spa

G4 5 av Saramartel, Antibes le1932hotelspa.com · €€

This Art Deco hotel is the place to eat well. Its breakfast spread is worthy of a royal banquet and its rooftop restaurant serves a sumptuous tapas menu. Other perks include spacious rooms, attentive staff and a rooftop pool offering sunset views over Cap d'Antibes.

Alpes-de-Haute-Provence

L'Hippocampe Volonne

E2 7 rue de la Durance, Volonne l-hippocampe.com · €

This campsite is all about choice. Choice of lodgings, with villas, mobile homes, lodges, pre-erected tents and pitches. Choice of swimming spots, including a lagoon and multiple pools. And choice of activities, with a long list of sports clubs and evening entertainment.

Plaines-Provence Spa & Sauna

E2 399 rte des Plaines, Champtercier 06 78 15 61 77 · €

Tucked away in verdant countryside, these three *gîtes* – located in the outhouses of a 19th-century farmhouse – are the perfect place to retreat from modern life. Kick back with a book on one of the patio areas or relax in the spa, sauna and Jacuzzi (book for private hire).

Domaine de la Mautanne

D3 740 blvd François Billoux, Sainte-Tulle lamautanne.com · €

Found in the town of Sainte-Tulle, this estate comes into its own in lavender season, when nearby fields turn a deep purple. It's worth visiting whatever the season, though, thanks to its serene rooms, super-spacious apartments and excellent bistro-style restaurant.

Le Moulin du Château

E4 99 chemin d'Albiosc, St-Laurent-du-Verdon moulin-du-chateau.com · €€

This spot scores points for its historic charm (it's set in a former 17th-century olive mill) and its location, not far from the Gorges du Verdon. But where it really shines is with its eco-credentials: seasonal, organic produce is served in the restaurant; there are on-site EV charging points; and all cleaning products are eco-friendly. There are bicycles for hire, too.

Vaucluse

Hôtel Crillon-le-Brave

C2 pl de l'Église, Crillon-le-Brave crillonlebrave.com · €€€

Nestled amid the picturesque village of Crillon-le-Brave, this palatial hotel is made up of a collection of 17th- and 18th-century buildings, all built from sandy-coloured local stone and liberally blanketed with Virginia creeper. Rooms are upmarket yet down-to-earth, with warm tones and lots of linen, and the service is first class.

Cabanes des Grands Cépages

B3 2061 chemin des Pompes, Sorgues cabanesdesgrandscepages.com · €€

It may be only a short distance from the pretty town of Sorgues, but this eco-retreat feels wonderfully secluded. Here, choose from floating, stilted or camouflaged cabins, each one made using PEFC-certified wood from French forests and containing unique items made by local artisans. Activities are of the slow-tourism variety: cycling, fishing and yoga, to name but a few.

L'Oasis d'Avignon

S4 10 imp du Rhône, Villeneuve-lès-Avignon hotel-oasis-avignon.com · €

A hotel for (almost) the price of a hostel? That's a steal. Even more so, since the rooms here are comfortable and light-filled, and Avignon's old town is just a 15-minute walk away. Another highlight is the fantastic view over the famous Palais des Papes from across the River Rhône.

INDEX

Page numbers in **bold** refer to main entries.

D

E

F

M

N

O

P

Q

R

PHRASE BOOK

In an Emergency

Help!	**Au secours!**	*oh sekoor!*
Stop!	**Arrêtez!**	*aret-ay!*
Call…	**Appelez…**	*apuh-lay…*
…a doctor!	**…un médecin!**	*…uñ medsañ!*
…an ambulance!	**…une ambulance!**	*…oon oñboo-loñs!*
…the police!	**…la police!**	*…lah poh-lees!*
…the fire brigade!	**…les pompiers!**	*…leh poñ-peeyay!*

Communication Essentials

Yes/No	**Oui/Non**	*wee/noñ*
Please	**S'il vous plaît**	*seel voo play*
Thank you	**Merci**	*mer-see*
Excuse me	**Excusez-moi**	*exkoo-zay mwah*
Hello	**Bonjour**	*boñzhoor*
Goodbye	**Au revoir**	*oh ruh-vwar*
Good night	**Bonsoir**	*boñ-swar*
What?	**Quel, quelle?**	*kel, kel?*
When?	**Quand?**	*koñ?*
Why?	**Pourquoi?**	*poor-kwah?*
Where?	**Où?**	*oo?*

Useful Phrases

How are you?	**Comment allez-vous?**	*kom-moñ talay voo?*
Very well	**Très bien**	*treh byañ*
Pleased to meet you.	**Enchanté de faire votre connaissance.**	*oñshoñ-tay duh fehr votr kon-ay-sans.*
Where is/are…?	**Où est/sont…?**	*oo ay/soñ…?*
Which way to…?	**Quelle est la direction pour…?**	*kel ay lah deer-ek-syoñ poor…?*
Do you speak English?	**Parlez-vous anglais?**	*par-lay voo oñg-lay?*
I don't understand.	**Je ne compr-ends pas.**	*zhuh nuh kom-proñ pah.*
I'm sorry.	**Excusez-moi.**	*exkoo-zay mwah.*

Useful Words

big	**grand**	*groñ*
small	**petit**	*puh-tee*
hot	**chaud**	*show*
cold	**froid**	*frwah*
good	**bon**	*boñ*
bad	**mauvais**	*moh-veh*
open	**ouvert**	*oo-ver*
closed	**fermé**	*fer-meh*
left	**gauche**	*gohsh*
right	**droit**	*drwah*
entrance	**l'entrée**	*l'on-tray*
exit	**la sortie**	*sor-tee*
toilet	**les toilettes**	*twah-let*

Shopping

How much is it?	**Ça fait combien?**	*sa fay kom-byañ?*
What time…	**A quelle heure…**	*ah kel urr…*
…do you open?	**…êtes-vous ouvert?**	*…et-voo oo-ver?*
…do you close?	**…êtes-vous fermé?**	*…et-voo fer-may?*
Do you have?	**Est-ce que vous avez?**	*es-kuh voo zavay?*
I would like …	**Je voudrais…**	*zhuh voo-dray…*
Do you take credit cards?	**Est-ce que vous acceptez les cartes de crédit?**	*es-kuh voo zaksept-ay leh kart duh krehdee?*
This one.	**Celui-ci.**	*suhl-wee-see.*
That one.	**Celui-là.**	*suhl-wee-lah.*
expensive	**cher**	*shehr*
cheap	**pas cher, bon marché**	*pah shehr, boñ mar-shay*
size, clothes	**la taille**	*tye*
size, shoes	**la pointure**	*pwañ-tur*

Types of Shop

antique shop	**le magasin d'antiquités**	*maga-zañ d'oñteekee-tay*
bakery	**la boulangerie**	*booloñ-zhuree*
bank	**la banque**	*boñk*
bookshop	**la librairie**	*lee-brehree*
cake shop	**la pâtisserie**	*patee-sree*
cheese shop	**la fromagerie**	*fromazh-ree*
chemist	**la pharmacie**	*farmah-see*
department store	**le grand magasin**	*groñ maga-zañ*
delicatessen	**la charcuterie**	*sharkoot-ree*
gift shop	**le magasin de cadeaux**	*maga-zañ duh kadoh*
greengrocer	**le marchand de légumes**	*mar-shoñ duh lay-goom*
grocery	**l'alimentation**	*alee-moñtasyoñ*
market	**le marché**	*marsh-ay*
newsagent	**le magasin de journaux**	*maga-zañ duh zhoor-no*
post office	**la poste, le bureau de poste, le PTT**	*pohst, booroh duh pohst, peh-teh-teh*
supermarket	**le supermarché**	*soo pehr-marshay*
tobacconist	**le tabac**	*tabah*
travel agent	**l'agence de voyages**	*l'azhoñs duh vwayazh*

Sightseeing

art gallery	**la galerie d'art**	*galer-ree dart*
bus station	**la gare routière**	*gahr roo-tee-yehr*
cathedral	**la cathédrale**	*katay-dral*
church	**l'église**	*l'aygleez*
garden	**le jardin**	*zhar-dañ*
library	**la bibliothèque**	*beebleeo-tek*
museum	**le musée**	*moo-zay*
railway station	**la gare (SNCF)**	*gahr (es-en-say-ef)*
tourist office	**l'office du tourisme**	*ohfees doo tooreesm*
town hall	**l'hôtel de ville**	*l'ohtel duh veel*

Staying in a Hotel

Do you have a vacant room?	**Est-ce que vous avez une chambre?**	*es-kuh voo-zavay oon shambr?*
I have a reservation.	**J'ai fait une réservation.**	*zhay fay oon rayzehrva-syoñ.*
single room	**la chambre à une personne**	*shambr ah oon pehr-son*
twin room	**la chambre à deux lits**	*shambr ah duh lee*
room with a bath, shower	**la chambre avec salle de bains, une douche**	*shambr avek sal duh bañ, oon doosh*

double room, with a double bed	**la chambre à deux personnes, avec un grand lit**	*shambr ah duh pehr-son, avek un gronñ lee*

Eating Out

Have you got a table?	**Avez-vous une table libre?**	*avay-voo oon tahbl duh leebr?*
I want to reserve a table.	**Je voudrais réserver une table.**	*zhuh voo-dray rayzehr-vay oon tahbl.*
The bill, please.	**L'addition, s'il vous plaît.**	*l'adee-syoñ seel voo play.*
Waitress/ waiter	**Madame, Mademoiselle/ Monsieur**	*mah-dam, mah-demwahzel/ muh-syuh*
menu	**le menu, la carte**	*men-oo, kart*
fixed-price menu	**le menu à prix fixe**	*men-oo ah pree feeks*
cover charge	**le couvert**	*koo-vehr*
wine list	**la carte des vins**	*kart-deh vañ*
glass	**le verre**	*vehr*
bottle	**la bouteille**	*boo-tay*
knife	**le couteau**	*koo-toh*
fork	**la fourchette**	*for-shet*
spoon	**la cuillère**	*kwee-yehr*
breakfast	**le petit déjeuner**	*puh-tee deh-zhuh-nay*
lunch	**le déjeuner**	*deh-zhuh-nay*
dinner	**le dîner**	*dee-nay*
main course	**le plat principal**	*plah prañsee-pal*
starter, first course	**l'entrée, le hors d'oeuvre**	*l'oñ-tray, or-duhvr*
dish of the day	**le plat du jour**	*plah doo zhoor*
wine bar	**le bar à vin**	*bar ah vañ*
café	**le café**	*ka-fay*

Menu Decoder

baked	**cuit au four**	*kweet oh foor*
beef	**le boeuf**	*buhf*
beer	**la bière**	*bee-yehr*
boiled	**bouilli**	*boo-yee*
bread	**le pain**	*pan*
butter	**le beurre**	*burr*
cake	**le gâteau**	*gah-toh*
cheese	**le fromage**	*from-azh*
chicken	**le poulet**	*poo-lay*
chips	**les frites**	*freet*
chocolate	**le chocolat**	*shoko-lah*
coffee	**le café**	*kah-fay*
dessert	**le dessert**	*deh-ser*
duck	**le canard**	*kanar*
egg	**l'oeuf**	*l'uf*
fish	**le poisson**	*pwah-ssoñ*
fresh fruit	**le fruit frais**	*frwee freh*
garlic	**l'ail**	*l'eye*
grilled	**grillé**	*gree-yay*
ham	**le jambon**	*zhoñ-boñ*
ice, ice cream	**la glace**	*glas*
lamb	**l'agneau**	*l'anyoh*
lemon	**le citron**	*see-troñ*
fresh lemon juice	**le citron pressé**	*see-troñ presseh*
meat	**la viande**	*vee-yand*
milk	**le lait**	*leh*
mineral water	**l'eau minérale**	*l'oh meeney-ral*
oil	**l'huile**	*l'weel*
onions	**les oignons**	*leh zonyoñ*
orange juice	**l'orange pressée**	*l'oroñzh presseh*
pepper	**le poivre**	*pwavr*
pork	**le porc**	*por*
potatoes	**les pommes de terre**	*pom duh tehr*
rice	**le riz**	*ree*
roast	**rôti**	*row-tee*
salt	**le sel**	*sel*
sausage	**la saucisse**	*sohsees*
seafood	**les fruits de mer**	*frwee duh mer*
snails	**les escargots**	*leh zes-kar-goh*
soup	**la soupe, le potage**	*soop, poh-tazh*
steak	**le bifteck, le steak**	*beef-tek, stek*
sugar	**le sucre**	*sookr*
tea	**le thé**	*tay*
vegetables	**les légumes**	*lay-goom*
vinegar	**le vinaigre**	*veenaygr*
water	**l'eau**	*l'oh*
red wine	**le vin rouge**	*vañ roozh*
white wine	**le vin blanc**	*vañ bloñ*

Numbers

0	**zéro**	*zeh-roh*
1	**un, une**	*uñ, oon*
2	**deux**	*duh*
3	**trois**	*trwah*
4	**quatre**	*katr*
5	**cinq**	*sañk*
6	**six**	*sees*
7	**sept**	*set*
8	**huit**	*weet*
9	**neuf**	*nerf*
10	**dix**	*dees*
11	**onze**	*oñz*
12	**douze**	*dooz*
13	**treize**	*trehz*
14	**quatorze**	*katorz*
15	**quinze**	*kañz*
16	**seize**	*sehz*
17	**dix-sept**	*dees-set*
18	**dix-huit**	*dees-weet*
19	**dix-neuf**	*dees-nerf*
20	**vingt**	*vañ*
30	**trente**	*tront*
40	**quarante**	*karoñt*
50	**cinquante**	*sañkoñt*
60	**soixante**	*swasoñt*
70	**soixante-dix**	*swasoñt-dees*
80	**quatre-vingts**	*katr-vañ*
90	**quatre-vingt-dix**	*katr-vañ-dees*
100	**cent**	*soñ*
1,000	**mille**	*meel*

Time

one minute	**une minute**	*oon mee-noot*
one hour	**une heure**	*oon urr*
half an hour	**une demi-heure**	*urr duh-me urr*
one day	**un jour**	*urr zhorr*
Monday	**lundi**	*luñ-dee*
Tuesday	**mardi**	*mar-dee*
Wednesday	**mercredi**	*mehrkruh-dee*
Thursday	**jeudi**	*zhuh-dee*
Friday	**vendredi**	*voñdruh-dee*
Saturday	**samedi**	*sam-dee*
Sunday	**dimanche**	*dee-moñsh*

ACKNOWLEDGMENTS

This edition updated by

Contributor Anna Richards

Senior Editors Keith Drew, Kiron Gill

Senior Designer Vinita Venugopal

Project Editors Rachel Laidler, Anuroop Sanwalia

Editors Abhidha Lakhera, Sarah Mathew

Project Art Editor Bharti Karakoti

Proofreader Kathryn Glendenning

Indexer Helen Peters

Deputy Picture Research Manager Virien Chopra

Assistant Picture Research Administrator Manpreet Kaur

Rights and Permissions Specialist Priya Singh

Publishing Assistant Simona Velikova

Jacket Designers Bharti Karakoti, Katie Cavanagh

Jacket Picture Researcher Harriet Mills

Project Cartographer Ashif

Senior Cartographic Editor James MacDonald

Cartography Manager Suresh Kumar

Pre-production Coordinator Tanveer Zaidi

Pre-production Designer Rajdeep Singh

Pre-production Image Coordinator Jagtar Singh

Pre-production Image Editor Ashok Kumar

Pre-production Manager Balwant Singh

Pre-production Image Manager Pankaj Sharma

Production Controller Kariss Ainsworth

Deputy Managing Editor Dharini Ganesh

Managing Editor Beverly Smart

Managing Art Editors Gemma Doyle, Priyanka Thakur

Editorial Director Hollie Teague

Art Director Maxine Pedliham

Publishing Director Georgina Dee

DK would like to thank the following for their contribution to the previous editions: Dana Facaros, Robin Gauldie, Anthony Peregrine, Tristan Rutherford.

The publisher would like to thank the following for their kind permission to reproduce their photographs:

Key: a-above; b-below/bottom; c-center; f-far; l-left; r-right; t-top.

123RF.com: server 107t.

Adobe Stock: Bruno 23crb; oleg_p_100 110.

Alamy Stock Photo: Jon Arnold 12br, 41t, 98; Art Kowalsky 107b; blickwinkel / P. Royer 63; Boizet / Alpaca / Andia 121; Roland Bouvier 94b; BSR Agency 10bl; BTWImages 49b; Cavan Images / Christophe Launay 97; Chronicle 8, 10tl; Classic Image 9tl, 9cr, 12crb, 23br; dpa picture alliance 62t; Andrew Duke 134b; Endless Travel 64–65, 103; © Fine Art Images / Heritage Images 50; Ciscardi Gabriel 129b; GL Archive 11t; Hemis / Bertrand Gardel 24–25b, 104, 129t; Cavalier Michel / Hemis.fr 13clb, 16cla, 21t, 56, 137; Chaput Franck / Hemis.fr 124–125t, 125b; Charton Franck / Hemis.fr 62b; Gardel Bertrand / Hemis.fr 82t; Guy Christian / Hemis.fr 12cr, 27tr, 27cla; Hughes Herv / Hemis.fr 68; Leclercq Olivier / Hemis.fr 76t; Leroy Francis / Hemis.fr 54; Martelet Christian / Hemis.fr 19; Mattes René / Hemis.fr 5, 46, 90, 93, 132b; Moirenc Camille / Hemis.fr 1, 13cla, 70, 94–95t, 135; Montico Lionel / Hemis.fr 25t; Rieger Bertrand / Hemis.fr 45t, 99, 117t, 118t; Ruth Hofshi 131; Peter Horree 49t; imageBROKER / Daniel Schoenen 36cla; Imago 22; Imago / Offenberg 87; IMAGO / Peter Seyfferth finephotoart.org 66; Index / Heritage Images 51b; John Kellerman 40, 44, 123t; Hervé Lenain 61t; Marco Maraviglia 15clb; Hilke Maunder 71t; Angus McComiskey 101; Tuul and Bruno Morandi 43, 77t; James Moy 75t; Gerard Sioen / Onlyfrance.fr 53t; Robert Palomba / Onlyfrance.fr 13cl; Panther Media Global / Marco Rubino / marcorubino 13cl (8), 102t; Paul Quayle 73b; RealyEasyStar / Paolo Bolla 123b; Robert Harding World Imagery 26; Shawshots 10cl; Mats Silvan 23bl; The Picture Art Collection 9tr; travelstock44.de / Juergen Held 105, 108; Universal Images Group North America LLC / DeAgostini / DEA / G. DAGLI ORTI 23cb; Universal Images Group North America LLC / DeAgostini / EA / SANTINI / D'ALESSIO 71b; Belle Vue 47; YG-Tavel-Photos 88–89t; Didier Zylberyng 9br.

AWL Images: Marco Bottigelli 11b; ClickAlps 24cla; Guy Edwardes 72–73t; Hans Georg Eiben 29t, 36br, 79; Neil Farrin 20, 28, 29b, 31, 55, 81, 88b; Roland Gerth 37; Susanne Kremer 21b; Jason Langley 45b; Tom Mackie 12cra; Tim Mannakee 102b; PhotoFVG 13tl.

Bacon: 115.

Bridgeman Images: 10tr.

Chocolaterie Bernard Castelain: 134t.

Depositphotos Inc: bernjuer 69b.

Dreamstime.com: Andrei Antipov 67; Bumbleedee 109; Sorin Colac 6–7; Daliu80 130; Dudlajzov 61b; Emicristea 126; Alexandre Fagundes De Fagundes 27tl; Evgeniy Fesenko 111; Sergio Formoso 132t; Francoisroux 69t; Werner Lerooy 91; Chris Mouyiaris 14, 114; Michael Mulkens 112; Marketa Novakova 57; ...e Sohm 48; Nickolay Stanev 52–53b; Dmytro ...urkov 117b; Larysa Uhryn 13bl; Emily Wilson ...–35t; Xantana 38–39; Znm 127.

...agonard Parfumeur: 16cr, 118–119b.

...etty Images: AFP / Gerard Julien 75b; Moment ... Cyrille Gibot 76–77b; Moment / zpagistock 133; ...hotodisc / P. Eoche 27cra; Reitz / ullstein bild ...t.

...etty Images / iStock: AsianDream 96; ...+ / aluxum 35b; E+ / Deejpilot 15bl; E+ / ...mgorthand 17; Kirk Fisher 120; marako85 58–59; travelview 15cb; Aleh Varanishcha 32–33; Rafael_Wiedenmeier 82b; Alan York 15crb.

Île Degaby: Mickael Bandassak 84.

Monte-Carlo S.B.M. Hotels and Casinos: 113.

Shutterstock.com: Francesco Bonino 83; Cavan-Images 16cra; Kirk Fisher 30, 41b; Tommy Larey 74.

Sofitel Marseille Vieux Port - Les Trois Forts: 85.

Cover Images:

Front and Spine: **AWL Images:** Susanne Kremer; *Back:* **Alamy Stock Photo:** Jon Arnold tr; dpa picture alliance tl; **AWL Images:** Neil Farrin cl.

Sheet Map Cover Image:

AWL Images: Susanne Kremer.

Illustrator: Chris Orr & Associates.

A NOTE FROM DK

The rate at which the world is changing is constantly keeping the DK travel team on our toes. While we've worked hard to ensure that this edition of Provence and the Côte d'Azur is accurate and up-to-date, we know that opening hours alter, standards shift, prices fluctuate, places close and new ones pop up in their stead. So, if you notice we've got something wrong or left something out, we want to hear about it. Please get in touch at travelguides@dk.com

Within each Top 10 list in this book, no hierarchy of quality or popularity is implied. All 10 are, in the editor's opinion, of roughly equal merit.

First edition 2002

Published in Great Britain by Dorling Kindersley Limited, DK, 20 Vauxhall Bridge Road, London SW1V 2SA

The authorised representative in the EEA is Dorling Kindersley Verlag GmbH. Arnulfstr. 124, 80636 Munich, Germany

Published in the United States by DK Publishing, 1745 Broadway, 20th Floor, New York, NY 10019, USA

26 27 28 29 10 9 8 7 6 5 4 3 2 1

A CIP catalog record for this book is available from the British Library.

A catalog record for this book is available from the Library of Congress.

ISSN: 1479-344X
ISBN: 978 0 2417 8333 7

Printed and bound in China

www.dk.com

MIX
Paper | Supporting responsible forestry
FSC™ C018179

This book was made with Forest Stewardship Council™ certified paper – one small step in DK's commitment to a sustainable future.
Learn more at **www.dk.com/uk/information/sustainability**